SPIKE MILLIGAN

THE FAMILY ALBUM

SPIKE MILLIGAN

THE FAMILY
ALBUM

Virgin

AN ILLUSTRATED
AUTOBIOGRAPHY

First published in 1999 by
Virgin Publishing Ltd
Thames Wharf Studios
Rainville Road
London W6 9HA

Copyright (c) 1999, Spike Milligan Productions Ltd

A catalogue record for this book is available from
the British Library.

ISBN 1 85227 886 2

Printed and bound in Great Britain by Butler and
Tanner Ltd, Frome and London.

Art direction and design by Derek Slatter,
Katherine Spokes and Emma Murray at Slatter Anderson.
Photography by RSA Photography

Additional photographs courtesy of Adrian Rigelsford,
Hulton Getty and PA News Photo Library.

CONTENTS

FOREWORD

I have unexpected pressure on me to
write a foreword for this book. I resent
this, given that I wrote the whole
bloody book by hand and I am still
writing for the pleasure of the publisher.

I can't wish him well, I can only hope
that he explodes sitting on a railway
train going to work, and his bits are
distributed to all his fellow passengers
as souvenirs.

I refuse to write any more.

Goodbye forever,

Spike Milligan

THE KETTLEBANDS AND THE MILLIGANS

Florence Kettleband

My Grandfather, Alfred Henry Kettleband, was born in Agra, India on 13 January 1869 and baptised on 6 February by Chaplain W H Tribe, C of E.

He enlisted as a Boy Soldier on 27 February 1884 in the Royal Artillery, 4th Brigade – he was just 14 years old. He gave his family home as Forton Road, Gosport, and his mother's name as Mary. Alfred's bride to be, although he didn't yet know it, was Margaret Glora Burnside, born 22 May 1868, Gosport. Her father was Regimental Sergeant Major John Burnside, Royal Artillery, her mother Margaret Ryan. Little Margaret went to school at the Convent of Virgo Fidelis in Upper Norwood in London and for her confirmation in 1882, she chose the name Mary. Margaret was then sent to Paris as a governess, to the family of the Marquis de Vogue.

Entire Kettleband family
including little Alfred Jnr. Soon
he'd be dead.

The family had four sons: Henri, Raymond, Felix and Pierre. Henri and Pierre were later killed in World War I. One memorable day during Margaret's time in Paris came on 28 December 1886 when she was 18. A gentleman friend took her to the square of La Roquette where at 7.31 a.m. Haro (alias Mendoza) was beheaded. Merry Christmas, Margaret.

1890

Margaret met Alfred when she was living back in England at 43 Jackson Street, Woolwich. How they met, I don't know – perhaps a regimental ball. Margaret would be quite a catch for a young soldier with her father being Regimental Sergeant Major. Their courting days would have been around 1890 – 1891

and Alfred might have taken Margaret to the Woolwich Empire – the working class entertainment of the day – to see acts like G. H. Elliot, Dan Leno or Eugene Stratton.

1892

Their wedding took place on 5 March 1892 at St Peter's Catholic Church, Woolwich, but things would not have gone entirely smoothly.

Margaret, remember, was a practising Catholic, and practice makes perfect. Alfred was C of E – a barbarian.

The day before the wedding, Alfred became a Catholic, baptised in St Peter's Church. There is no record of honeymoon, if ever there was one, but my mother recalled them living at 52

Above:
My Great Grandmother,
Mary Kettleband.

Jackson Street. There was born a girl later that year, but alas she died (my mother said) of convulsions brought on by overfeeding. What a terrible thing for a young married couple.

1893

Another girl was born in July 1893 – Florence Mary Winifred – my mother. She was baptised at St John's in Woolwich and her father's occupation was then given as 'Labourer', although he was still in the army.

Still in the army, that is, until 26 February 1896 when he was discharged. Termination of Engagement. He did, however, continue with his job at the Woolwich Arsenal and in August 1896, he re-enlisted in the Army Reserve, Royal Artillery.

They were still doing 'it' as there was born a boy in August, Bertram William Herbert. Florence and Alfred took them to the circus and to pantomimes, enjoying a peaceful family life.

October 1898

Oh, dear. The Boer War started.

December 1898

Oh, dear. Alfred was recalled to the colours.

Below:
My future mother with her mother.

Left:
Florence, Margaret and Bertram
prior to their departure for India

Below:
Alfred Jnr's birth certificate.

He was posted to 7 Depot Ammunition Column. That seems safe enough, but by April he had been appointed Sergeant Trumpeter and posted to I Brigade, Staff Division, Royal Field Artillery, South Africa. He served in the Boer War and had the South Africa medal with Johannesburg Orange Free State, Cape Colony clasps and the Long Service and Good Conduct medals.

August 1901

Alfred was discharged: Termination of Engagement on 15 August. He waited a couple of months then . . . 14 October

1901 he re-enlisted in 107 Royal Field Artillery, Regular Army.

1902

The Boer War ended and Alfred was sent to a military depot in Ahmednagar, India. He was later joined here by Margaret, Florence and Bertram. My mother recalled that they travelled to India on a troop ship. Many of the women and children had lice in their hair. To make matters worse, on arrival in Ahmednagar, they were hit by a cyclone and a plague of locusts!

1903

Alfred was posted to 42 Brigade, 107 R.F.A. in Kirkee, India. They were still doing it. A girl was born on 21 October 1904 and nine days later Alfred was discharged. Termination of Engagement. In November the baby girl was baptised Eileen Patricia May at St Ignatius', the Catholic church in Kirkee.

1906

In January Margaret Burnside, my Great Grandmother, died in Woolwich. Margaret and Alfred, however, went on doing it and in October a boy was born, baptised Alfred Henry at St Ignatius' in Kirkee.

1910

Alfred was by now in charge

Right:
Betram and his father outside St Ignatius' Church.

of a mineral-water factory in Kirkee. In a letter of reference dated 6 October 1913, Lt Colonel J. H. Tillit described my grandfather as 'An honest very smart man he has been i/c the Boys Depot, and i/c Mineral Water Factory for three years. A thoroughly reliable man.' Thoroughly reliable and still doing it.

1911

In January a boy was born and baptised the next month in St Ignatius' as Hugh Clarence. In May Sgt Trumpeter Kettleband is discharged. Why? I don't know – he was already discharged in 1905 – perhaps it didn't take.

1912

Alfred Henry Jnr was admitted to the Station Hospital. His sister Florence stayed with him. Nine days later, at 9.45 a.m., Alfred Jnr died. On his death certificate it said 'Tonsillitis' but in fact it was Vincent's Angina. My mother told me he died screaming in her arms.

Leo Milligan
1912

L/Bombardier Leo Milligan arrived in India. Why? He had been forced to join the army at the age of 14 by his father.

1890

He was born on 13 June in Holborn Street, Sligo, in Ireland. His father was William Milligan, a Royal Artillery

Above:
What's it all about, Alfie?

Below:
My father to be.

Top:
Leo Milligan in the bloody army.

Above:
The house where my father was born in Sligo.

Wheelwright. His mother was Elizabeth Higgins. Leo was due to be baptised Percy Marmaduke, alas, at Sligo Cathedral. There the bloody fool of a priest said, 'Why not name him after the dear Pope?' So he became Leo Alphonso.

1896

The family moved to London and took up residence in a mansion block in Poplar. Leo's father was employed in some sort of capacity as a janitor and was responsible for the gas lighting along the corridors, a job he delegated to his sons – he had four boys (help!). He also doubled as a stage hand at the Poplar Hippodrome. The Queen's Theatre stage door faced on to the building where the Milligans lived and my father saw all the stars arriving. He developed a love for the theatre which he never lost, leading him as a boy to becoming a 'super' (an extra). He appeared with names like Kate Karney and Leonora Mortimer, with whom he played the kid with the crutch in *Paying The Penalty*. He was an extra with *Artimus* in the role of a small boy soldier. He said he had to march up and down and do some tumbling.

Leo's local school was Wade Street, ruled by Headmaster McGinty but, at some point, he also went to the Steadman School of Dancing, then . . .

1904

. . . his father forced him to join the bloody army. Leo enlisted in 14 Royal Artillery at Shrapnel Barracks, No 1 Depot, Woolwich on 13 October. Army No 1036429. Early next year, Leo was posted to Brook Street Barracks in Birmingham. A cousin, Jeannie McDonald, said that he wanted to marry her but that, because they were cousins, his mother forbade it. He went to see her to say goodbye.

1906

Leo was promoted to trumpeter at a practice camp in Twasfynydd in Wales.

1909

Leo boxed for the regiment and the regiment was sent to Fermoy in Ireland.

1910

Leo was promoted to Bombardier. In September he did a soft-shoe shuffle and

Top Left:
All in the bloody army.

Bottom Left:
Leo, still entertaining as a clown at a fête in Birmingham.

Below:
Leo boxed for the regiment and would later teach me.

first-rate step dancer and singer. At another concert in December he sang 'Cindy You Is Ma Dream', again in 'coon' make-up. He bought a copy of 'Lily Of Laguna' and copied the figure on the cover for his costume and make-up. He also appeared in a character sketch and started using the stage name Leo Gann.

1911

Leo was posted to Woolwich to start an equestrian course. In September he entered a talent contest at the Imperial Palace, Canning Town, again using the stage name Leo Gann.

sang 'My Little Octoroon' in 'coon' make-up (terribly politically incorrect now, but that's what they called it then) at a concert in New Barracks in Fermoy. Despite being in the army, Leo had become a

Above:
By now he was using the stage name Leo Gann.

Far right:
Leo in what was known as 'coon' make-up.

He won and was booked to do a week at the Imperial Palace. Around this time he also became sweet on a ballet dancer who changed her name from Hilda Munnings to the more exotic Lydia Sokolova.

LYDIA SOKOLOVA

farewell concert in New Barracks where he did the Cubanola Glide with Driver Waddle. Farewell concert? Yes, they were posted to India, sailing on the SS *Plassey* on 14 December. He said, 'On Christmas Day we were given an orange.' All his life he wanted sympathy and said this to get it. The fact is that on 25 December they were at the port of Suez where all kinds of fruit was available and could be bought very cheap!

By November he was back in Fermoy with the regiment, playing at a

1912

On 3 January there was a death on board. The four-year-old daughter of Corporal Coleridge was buried at sea.

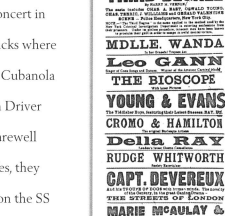

Top Left:
On the Equestrian course shovelling horse shit.

Left:
Lydia Sokolova, but on a post-card to Leo she signs it 'Hilda'

Above:
Framed copy of Play Bill for Leo's Imperial Palace performance.

Right:
Doing the Cubanola Glide with Driver Waddle.

They arrived at Bombay and entrained at Victoria Terminus for Kirkee, HQ of Southern Command on 4 January. Next day they were in barracks in Kirkee and the scene was set for my mother and father's great romance.

Leo fell in love with Florence Kettleband after hearing her playing the organ and singing in the church choir at St Ignatius'. She had a trained contralto voice. He always said, 'I fell in love with her voice.'

Leo's stage career continued with a concert for the 20th Brigade R. F. A. Kirkee in the Royal Artillery theatre. By now they were all kitted out in 'walking out whites'.

Corporal Coleridge on the water
Lost his four year baby daughter
He of the 8th Rifles
How the thought of that day stifles
Little girl of no first name
Life is lost before it came.

　　　　　Spike Milligan

Left:
Amazing transformation with 'walking out whites'.

The Regimental Dance in the summer of that year was held outdoors on the tennis court. Canvas was stretched over the court and French chalk worked into the surface to make it smooth for dancing. Sgt Trumpeter Kettleband wore full dress uniform. My mother said he had the first dance with his wife and the second dance with her.

From June to September, Leo toured India with The Gems. How did he get away with it? And on his return he was promoted to full Bombardier!

For Christmas that year Florence gave Leo a prayer book.

REGIMENTAL THEATRE,
TO-NIGHT !   TO-NIGHT !

THE GEMS'
Starring Engagement
— OF —
≈ Leo Gann ≈
America's Premier Ragtime
Comedian and Dancer.

Don't Fail to See !
THIS TALENTED ARTISTE
— IN HIS —
WORLD RENOWNED MAY DANCES.

First Tour in India
— AND —
THE FAR EAST.

1913

Leo and Florence became engaged, but he was still treading the boards. In June he appeared at the Bombay Novelty Theatre – a two-week engagement as Leo Gann. A fortnight later, The Gems are topping the bill at Poona Gymkhana Club.

Above:
An engagement ring wearing my mother.

Right:
Top billing, but already he was going bald.

Hotel. There was no wedding photo. Now where would they have spent their honeymoon night?

Leo was listed to go overseas and his battery was sent to a departure camp in Bombay prior to being shipped to Mesopotamia. By April they were in action.

Top Left:
Touring India bullock cart style.

Left:
Leo beats baldness by having his head shaved at a departure camp in Bombay.

1915

In his diary, Leo also said that they were at the Battle of Shaibah which was in April 1915 in Mesopotamia. He was promoted to Sergeant in the field. In June he was taken ill with a high temperature. He was taken by ambulance from the Kirkuk river to Ahwaz, 'Bounced over sand hills with the dysentery of the patient above dripping down on me.' Always looking

1914

In March, with the Great War looming, Leo and Florence were married by Registrar in Room 13 of the Poona

Top:
Fire!

Above:
The hospital ship on which Leo travelled from Basra to Bombay.

Right:
Florence on her way to see the patient with 'inflammation of the soft palate'.

for sympathy.

After 29 days a doctor diagnosed him as having 'Inflammation of the soft palate'! (I think he made this up). 'On discharge from hospital,' he said, 'I had a good meal that nearly killed me!' He spent three days at a base depot before being given passage on a hospital ship from Basra to Bombay. Eventually he

Excelcior Kinema

—: 0 :—

Commencing Wed. 16th August 1916.

(3 NIGHTS ONLY 3)

MORE STARS!   MORE STARS!!

Special engagement for a few nights only

MISS GEORGIE DEVOE

"   "   "

The lady Patter Comedian

in

FEMININE IMPRESSIONS!

The Quick fire sister, Letter there is not a deaf woman and
when this lady is on the stage ! some ladies talk 20 the dozen

This Lady Talks Fifty!

For a few Nights only

CHARLOTTA
CHARLOTTA
CHARLOTTA

The Versatile Dancer, from Clog to Classical Dancer,

International Dances !
American Dances !
Continental Dances !

SEE Her Celebrated Charlie Chapplin Dance !

NEW DANCES EVERY OTHER NIGHT !

Come to the EXCELCIOR !

The

Theatre of Star Attractions.

Coming!   Coming!!

Sat. Sun. Mon. Tues.

August 19th 20th 21st 22nd

G. WENNIE GORDON.

—: 0 :—

Versatile Connediente Singer of Ballads, Patriotic and
Chorus Songs.

LEO   GANN

—: 0 :—

American Ragtime Comedian Expert Mat,
Buck and Skipping Rope Dancer.

ALSO

GORDON AND GANN

—: 0 :—

In a "Repertoir" of Screamingly Funny Sketches, including

"Fun Round a Sentry Box"

A Laugh From Start to Finish.

DON'T MISS THIS ? ? PROGRAMME.

arrived at the military hospital in Ghopuri, Poona. Florence visited him there on horseback.

Once Leo had recovered sufficiently, he travelled back to Kirkee in the Rajah of Agalote's car (!?)

Florence's family then insisted that they had a proper church wedding. This took place at St Patrick's in Poona on 19 August. The ceremony was performed by Father O. Ehrle – a German! Again, no wedding photo.

While Leo was in Mesopotamia he had written the lyrics of a song:

It is sunset on the palm trees,
And a long day's work is done,
I am only waiting to see
My pretty village flower

She passes here at sunset
To draw water from the well
Her glances mean she loves me
Truly I can tell.

My lips have never uttered
What my heart prompts me to say
But still I am confident
She'll be my bride one day

God he was a romantic fool!

My mother's recollection of the wedding was that they were driven in a horse drawn Victoria. She wore a white wedding dress and Leo was in 'walking out whites'. As a wedding present she was given a gold watch and her wedding ring was made from gold sovereigns. Sgt Trumpeter Kettleband didn't attend the wedding as he had been posted to Ghora Daka, a real arsehole station.

My God – on their wedding night they did a concert in Bombay!

Left:
Honeymoon night!

Right:
Florence and Leo in *Fun Round A Sentry Box.*

GROWING UP IN INDIA

1916

In January Leo was posted to 77 Battery at Jhamsai. Here he became riding master and gave instruction on equestrian drill. He also formed a concert party.

1917

War was still raging, but in India it didn't seem to matter. Leo and Florence had photos taken for Christmas. This year they were to-ing and fro-ing between Jhamsai and Rawlpindi until he was promoted to Quartermaster Sergeant and posted to Ahmednagar.

He recalled, 'I was given a lame Bombardier as a clerk. He stuttered. When he typed he stuttered. He would type "w-w-w-w-station, s-s-s-s-staff". He reported sick, saying that typing made him dizzy. Every morning I left our quarters listening to your mother

Florence and Leo, Christmas
1917. They distributed this
photo to the family.

vomiting with morning sickness. I couldn't help her, I had to be on time at the depot. Then a guardian angel appeared. The lady next door popped in to see your mother. "You poor thing," she said. "Is no one helping you?" From then on she kept a constant watch over her pregnancy'

I was causing trouble already!

'Some weeks before you were born, Florence was transferred to the maternity ward in the military hospital. It was bloody miles away from the depot!'

1918

I arrived on April 16. The strain of nursing me wore my parents out. 'You never stopped bloody screaming,' was how they put it. Eventually Mrs Margaret Kettleband joined them to help manage me. Along with her came Eileen and Hughie. The stress my father suffered was grim – he was starting to lose his hair! The torrid heat of India plus the effect of me screaming caused my mother to lose so much weight that the Medical Officer recommended a six month holiday in the United Kingdom. My

Left:
The camp in Ahmednagar.

Below:
Me and my mother both wearing dresses.

Above:
Notice of my arrival.

Right:
Me occupying my mother's lap and life.

father was to travel as 'nurse' to England.

Soldiers suffer terrible withdrawal symptoms if they don't have anyone to shoot at, so to cure this, and to get away from screaming me, my father organised a hunting trip to far away Rui. During the hunt they shot black buck. It was a bit of a one-sided conflict with no reports of the black bucks ever returning fire, although our side did incur one casualty – my father had an attack of malaria. To help him recover, we moved to the cooler climate of Canoor where, again to get away from my continual screaming, my father took up golf. He was still losing his hair.

Left:
My mother trying to drown me in the bath between screams.

Above:
My father outside his office listening for my screams.

Above, Right:
Escaping from my screams.

Right:
My father playing golf and losing his hair.

My father struck it lucky. As well as the coming trip to England, the British Government was offering 1,000 Rupees for any soldier who wanted to serve on beyond his time. Meanwhile, I was being breast fed and starting to put on weight – whereas my mother was down to skin and bone. Before my father could strangle me, I was baptised Terence Alan on 30 April.

1919

It was July of the following year before we boarded the SS *Erinpura* (a hospital ship) at Bombay heading for six

months' leave in England. As the ship left Bombay, they could hear my screaming from the shore.

On 14 July at 0200 hours, calm sea, moonlit night, the SS *Erinpura* was shipwrecked on the Mushengera Reef off the Hamish Islands. There was no danger of the ship sinking as it was

WAR DIARY
for June 1919
INTELLIGENCE SUMMARY.

Voyage of AT Eings

Left:
The ship's log entry relating to the shipwreck.

Below:
New occupants, Mustapha Barracks, 1919.

stuck fast on the reef.

The passengers on board were all serving soldiers, wounded in the war. Many were sea-sick. My father said the ship was like 'a giant cuspidor.'

An SOS was sent out and the signal reached a destroyer from Aden – HMS *Topaz*. They took somewhere between 400 and 700 passengers to Aden. From there a steamer took us all to Alexandria in Egypt. We were transported in dirty buses to be billeted in the Mustapha Barracks.

Some days later we boarded the SS *Assaye* bound for Marseilles. The *Assaye* broke down and we were returned to Alexandria. On 20 July we re-boarded the *Assaye* and after docking in Marseilles we were billeted at the

Alexandria Egypt 1919

I don't know if you are aware but the Topaze took the passengers back to Aden & I have vivid memories of this as we had to steam very slowly being "top heavy" with the extra "Bods" on board.

Yours Sincerely
A.R. Rishman

12th November '76

Above:
A letter describing HMS Topaz as 'top heavy' with rescued passengers.

Right:
Chateau des Algalades. I screamed the place down.

wonderful Chateau des Algalades. I screamed the place down.

From Marseilles we were put on a train ('Cattle trucks,' said my father, looking for sympathy) to Le Havre, crossed the channel by ship to Southampton and boarded another train to Waterloo. The date was 8 August.

On arrival in London, we took a horse-drawn landau to Leo's mother's home in Poplar, where he had been as a boy. He said, 'My mother cried, my father wept. We were in need of sympathy and understanding. We were broke [what happened to the thousand Rupees, Dad?] and had had an extremely trying journey with a babe in arms. We were in need of comfort, affection and understanding.'

We stayed with a friend of my parents, George Guy, in Camden Town. Here we got comfort, affection and understanding. Leo got a job as a Tally Clerk in East India Docks. George Guy

1701 — Les Aygalades - Le Château

took Florence and Leo to many famous musicals including *Chu-Chin-Chow* with George Robie, and *The White Horse Inn.*

They had a bumper Christmas party that year but during the stay with the Guys, apart from comfort, affection and understanding, my mother alleged that George Guy's sister stole some of her jewellery, which had been given to her by Colonel Parbury in Poona. This must have made for an uncomfortable situation all round. I just carried on screaming.

1920

On March 27, Leo sailed back to India on the SS *Adolph Woerman*, a German ship taken as prize after World War I. The ship broke down and that evening he had to return to the Guys and my screaming. The ship finally set sail, delivering Leo to Port Said in Egypt on 10 April. He eventually reached Bombay on 22 April. He was then posted to 6 India Division, Kirkee, near Poona.

Back in England, things were getting worse. The Guys' children caught measles, I caught it and my mother caught it. She actually went blind and developed pneumonia and was admitted to the Canterbury Hospital in Sittingbourne. Weren't there enough hospitals in London? Aha – explanation! I was looked after by my Aunt Nance Barton, my mother's sister, who lived

Below:
The Guys, who gave the Milligans comfort, affection and understanding.

Above and Right:
The studio photographs we
had taken while in London.

in Sittingbourne.

My mother became so ill that Aunt
Nance telegraphed my grandmother in
Poona to inform her of Florence's
condition. When my father went to see
her, his first words
were, 'My Florrie's
dead, isn't she?'
Was this wishful
thinking? Did he
hope I had gone,
too, and that he
would never have
to suffer my
screaming again?

I myself was heartbroken at not
having my mother to scream at.
Apparently I wouldn't eat anything and
sobbed all day and half the night. The
rest of the night I spent screaming. I

Florence.

Terence

T.m suit in Tussore silk, made by his grandmother.

often wonder if this childhood incident had any effect on me growing up as a manic depressive.

My mother's sight was finally restored by a faith healer. At 3 a.m. one morning her fever broke. She recovered rapidly and was soon able to look after me again. She remembered the night she was discharged. There was heavy fog; it was only following my screaming that led her back to me.

For the rest of our time in England, we stayed with Aunt Nance.

Leo returned to the stage with his singing and dancing act, appearing in a concert in Kirkee on 26 November and another at the Regimental theatre of

10th Lincolnshire Regiment, Ghopuri, Poona on 23 December.

1921

My mother and I arrived back in Poona in the spring and they both appeared in concert at the Willingdon Soldiers' Club in Kirkee in April, in May Leo was raised to the Sublime Degree Master Mason, Kirkee. What a lot of balls – he didn't know what a trowel was! Despite this, in June he became Excellent Master in the Masons – more balls! They never did a thing for him!

Left:
Another photo from the studio in London.

Below:
The Kettleband family, front garden, Poona.

In contrast to the time recently spent in England, we Milligans went back to living the high life in India. There was a concert at the Napier Cinema in Poona, a concert at Poona Gymkhana and a fancy dress ball at Poona Gymkhana.

1922

More of the same! A swish concert at the Connaught Institute, Poona. Florence's dress was black satin with a rainbow of multi-colours at the top, her stockings were red. My father's top hat was bought from Dunn's in Oxford Street and my mother's black brocade shoes were from Rayner's in Bond Street. Where did they get the money?

Their life, I'm sad to say, was all huntin', shootin' and fishin'.

We often went for a drive through the beautiful Empress Gardens in a horse-drawn Victoria, pausing only to sniff the flowers, hit the driver and pose for a photograph with that prat, Major Parkinson, RAMC.

Far Left:
My mother and Aunty Eileen having lost all their money at the races and seeming very happy about it.

Left:
Huntin', shootin' and fishin' – Florence gets the bird.

Above:
Aunty Eileen and Major Parkinson RAMC, who is about to shoot himself in the foot.

Right:
Leo and Uncle Hughie go fishing. The fish is a Murrey River Cod. The others are not.

On 27 July BQMS Milligan and family were posted to Belgaum. My father wrote in his diary, 'Transferred to Belgaum. Terence's first misadventure was falling out of a tree. He went wandering round the married quarters where he was bitten by a dog.' I had to attend hospital in case I developed rabies. If I did, the dog would be shot and so would I.

In Belgaum I would roam the stables stroking the horses. My father's own horse was called Kitty. At breakfast she would put her head through the window for food.

In September, Florence, Eileen and Bert Kettleband appeared in a concert at the Mead Club along with Leo. More importantly, Leo

Above:

Leo and Florence sitting in the garden, Kirkee, 1921.

Below:

Evidence from the dog owner.

Please forgive me for writing to you as no doubt you get so many letters, but after hearing your Radio program on Monday 27th of January (Be my guest) when you said Belgaum India and that your father at that time was L.M. Sgt tough rider my mind went back to the year about 1922 - or 23. If I am not mistaken you were the little boy my dog had a bite at. Your leg the dogs name was (Bince) who was guarding my cookhouse and as you were playing around pushed the cookhouse door open hence the bite, Major de Warner ordered the dog to be shot but I being a woman & loved my dog pleaded for his life and won, we won a single Rtg belonging to the 18th Bde the rest were stationed

Ann Cooke (Rtrd)

bought me some rabbits which we kept under the house (it was on stilts).

One day when I came home (where on earth had I been?) one of the rabbits, a buck, escaped. My father tried to capture it by throwing a stone at it. He didn't capture it – he killed it. I cried a lot over that rabbit.

Top Right:
Florence and me sleeping outdoors in Kirkee, waited on hand and foot!

Above:
Spoilt me with toys and bearer.

1923

My grandfather, Alfred Henry Kettleband, was by now in very poor health, but he still went for walks in East street and in Main Street in Poona. On 19 May he went out, keen to buy a Royal Artillery tie to wear on Empire Day. While he was out he began to suffer chest pains. The pains became steadily worse and the family sent for a doctor to administer morphia.

Two days later my grandfather died. He was 52 and it was the day before Empire Day – what bad luck! Aunty Nelly Kettleband, wife of Bertram, was with him when he died. In her letters she said that she managed to give him some words of comfort. His aorta burst and blood poured out of his mouth, spilling out over Aunt Nelly's dress.

My own memory of him is him in bed in striped pyjamas. I recall him rising from his bed to shout at one of the servants. I also remember rudely awakening him from sleep one day by smacking him on the cheek, but in his eyes I could do no wrong. He always kept sweets for me under his pillow.

I also remember Christmas as being a very grand affair with Grandfather presiding over it. I would help my grandmother make chain decorations with coloured strips of paper and a mixture of flour-and-water paste. Christmas lunch was roast goose with vegetables. Grandfather wore full dress Royal Artillery blues buttoned right up to the neck with a white starched collar inside. He wore his Kings, Long Service and South African medals on his chest and on his sleeve were the gold service chevrons, gold sergeant's stripes. Down the side of his leg fitting trousers was a red stripe. Under the trousers he wore riding boots with small silver spurs. We all dressed up accordingly. Before dinner he said Grace, then three toasts – Queen Victoria! King Edward! King George! My glass was filled half with French red wine and half with water.

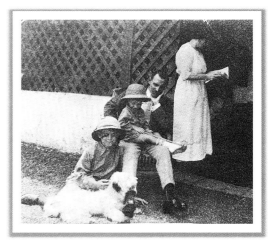

Above:
The only photograph of me with Alfred Kettleband. I am sitting on his lap. At the time, he was ill with heart trouble.

Left:
Grandfather's grave.

Above:
Leo dressed for his 'Piccadilly'
number.

Right:
My daughter Jane was in
Bombay and discovered the
Edward Theatre, where my
father had appeared, still in use!

Table was waited on by our bearer Thumby and the lunch ended with Christmas pudding set alight with flaming brandy. With cheese I was given a glass filled half with port and half with water. We all pulled crackers, put on funny hats and read the jokes. 'When is a horse not a horse? When it's turned into a field!' Then we retired to the drawing room where my mother played piano and sang. Hughie played the E-flat saxophone. My mother played piano while Eileen sang and played again for my grandparents to duet.

They played some rag-time on an old horned gramophone and I danced the Charleston. At eight o'clock I was sent to bed, too excited to sleep.

After I had finally dropped off, I woke in the middle of the night to see my mother and grandmother at the foot of my bed, having just put a pillow slip full of toys there. My mother said, 'Oh, Father Christmas has just gone out the window!' Oh, had he, now? The window was covered with narrow guage wire. I never doubted my mother, but

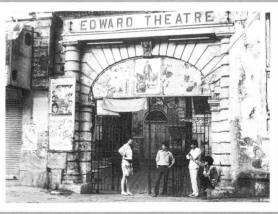

I did want to know how he got through the small hole in the chicken wire.

The abiding Christmas memory,

though, is of Grandfather sitting at the head of the table in all his finery.

He was laid to rest in St Sepulchre's Cemetery in Poona. His daughter Eileen threw herself on the grave and could not be consoled.

My mother recalled earlier, happier days when Alfred would rise every morning and say, 'Dog off chain – doors open – tea in pot!' At 6 a.m. he would have his horse brought by his syce (groom) Peshram and he would ride off to Garrisbrand. My mother said he would sometimes hit Peshram – a shocking way to treat anyone but it was the custom then. He would sing at the Sergeant's men's concerts, performing songs such as 'The Arab's Farewell To His Favourite Steed', 'Wrap Me Up In My Old Stable Jacket' or 'Just A Song At Twilight'.

Margaret Kettleband, still living in their house at 5 Climo Road in Poona, would have to survive on a widow's pension until she died, at the age of 83.

Above:
Florence and Leo, cowboys in the garden, Kirkee, 1921.

Above:
Happy family.

Below:
Florence with a dead deer.

Right:
Leo with another. Life in India was good for people, terrible for deer.

Prior to Alfred's death, Leo and Florence were still out there murdering the local wildlife. One trip took them to Patas where they stayed in a DAK bungalow, a house kept for visiting dignitaries. They received notice of Alfred's death by telegram in Belgaum. Shortly after Alfred's funeral, the engagement of Eileen to the twit Major Parkinson was celebrated at Muratores Restaurant in Poona.

It was around this time that I became a Boy Scout and did all the dib-dib-dob bit. The scouts attended the annual mounted-sports extravaganza on the Polo Ground in Belgaum where we watched my father indulging his cowboy obsession with a display of horsemanship. How many small boys have fathers who behave like this?

In December Leo was posted to Hyderabad, a real hell hole. We stayed in married quarters, a long line of buildings stretching off into the desert. I remember that it was incredibly hot there and I was struck down with a very high temperature. To keep our

Above:

The engagement party at Muratores. Standing left to right – Florence, Dr. Patel, Eileen, Major Parkinson, Leo. Seated – unknown, Hughie, Bertram and Nelly (Betram's wife)

This Page:
Leo performing equestrian tricks dressed as a cowboy and aided by my mother.

house, and me, cool, a gardener threw water on our cous-cous tatties, blinds made from slatted wood.

I was delirious and my parents sat up all night bathing me with cold water. My fever was diagnosed as clinical malaria and I would continue

to suffer from occasional bouts.

Up until the fevers started, I had been a bed wetter. I think it was a psychological reaction to my father being absent from home for so long on distant postings. Once, I awoke in the small hours (Small? They lasted all night!), took a woolly hat from my bedside and, unconcerned, widdled in it. To break me of the bed-wetting habit, my mother was told to sew a cotton reel in the back of my pyjamas. I still did it.

My last attack of malaria was over 15 years ago. I think I'm cured now. I'm cured of the bed wetting, too.

1924

In January Leo and Florence did a concert at the Majestic Cinema. Majestic? It was a ruin! Maybe it was the hellish heat, but I remember so many things crumbling into ruins there. I had a little metal train and I clearly recall running up to the farrier, Gunner Egham, to show it to him. While he was handling it, a wheel came off. I burst into tears. While I was crying, he quickly mended it on his anvil. What a fuss!

Above:

Mrs. Phillips outside the married quarters in Hyderabad. We were at the very end of this. We never met her.

And the train wasn't even my favourite toy. Between the ages of five and eight, I liked dolls. Father was very worried.

The heat became so bad that my mother and I were sent back to Poona where it was cooler. I then started school at the Convent of Jesus and Mary. There I was surrounded by pretty girls. One, a Persian, Fakri Shah, I fell in love with. This at least proved that playing with dolls was just a phase.

In March Leo was advised that he had been permitted to stay in service beyond 21 years, until July 1929. Five more years of the high life! The bad news was that he had been posted to III Brigade Artillery Force in Rangoon (the Ran Goon Show?), Burma. My mother and I were to stay behind with Gran Kettleband, Hughie and Eileen.

With my father away, life continued as usual at 5 Climo Road. My Uncle Hughie would sometimes take me swimming and I would ride with him on the back of his bike. He was very proud of his body and would stand before a mirror striking poses. I don't know why. He was a scrawny specimen.

I, meanwhile, was becoming a dirty little devil, peering through the keyhole to watch my Auntie Eileen having a bath! I was certainly becoming more aware of the opposite sex. I used to play with Tommy Basley who had a randy older sister, Louise, who would pull down her knickers, show me her

Below:
Me with Aunty Eileen, whose fanny I spied upon.

fanny and say, 'Is it all right, doctor?' It always looked all right to me.

I learned to speak Hindustani perfectly, playing hockey with the native children and flying kites using marndia string which was coated with ground glass in order to cut the strings of other kites and bring them down. An aggressive sport but fun, unlike the constant cruelty to animals that I witnessed as a child.

I knew a soldier whose job it was to shoot all the pariah dogs. I witnessed one he had shot. Alas, all he did was to make a hole in its backbone. It lay, still alive, on the ground. The soldier whistled to it and, my God, it wagged its tail. 'Please put it out of its misery,' I said, whereupon he blew its brains out. My good deed for the day, a bad

Above:

My childhood home, 5 Climo Road, as it is today…

one for the dog.

Directly opposite our house was the soldiers' barracks. There I witnessed something truly appalling. Some soldiers were trying to drown a pet monkey. They had filled a metal dustbin to the brim with water, put the monkey in and then put the lid on. When they lifted the lid the monkey was still alive. I didn't wait to see what happened.

There were good times with animals, too, of course. I once walked to the Poona race course. Inside the track were the Hindu bookies. I had been given six paisa (the lowest-value Indian coinage) by my grandmother. I started

Below:

... in ruins.

betting and, by God, I won. I kept winning. By the end of the day I had won three rupees! Some soldiers from the Ulster Rifles were at the races using binoculars to look at women in the stands. I said my mother and my Aunty Eileen were in the stands. One of the soldiers drew a picture of a fanny and asked if my aunty had one like it. I

knew she had, but I didn't tell them. After all, it was in the family.

At school, my teacher was Mother Fabien and I think she must have had a soft spot for me. Once I took a mouthful of water and sprayed it through a keyhole into a classroom. They soon tracked me down as the culprit but I was so beautiful (black, curly hair and bright blue eyes) that I was not punished. I'm sure the teacher fancied me, but the Mother Superior was immune to my charms. One day I fell in some mud and I was so sensitive about the girls at the

convent seeing me covered in mud that I climbed the school gates, caught a tonga (a kind of rickshaw) and went home. Next day when I got to the convent all the girls had been lined up. I was stood in front of them and screamed at by the Mother Superior. Fuck her for a start.

Every lunch time my ayah (she was a kind of maid or nanny) would walk two miles to the convent to bring me a hot meal in a three-tier carrier. The bottom one was hot water, the next a curry and the third rice. What a life!

1925

On Grandmother's pension day, a tonga with a white horse took us to the Post Office where she drew her pension, before going on to Poona bazaar where she bought me bull's-eyes and a *Tiger Tim* comic. On our return one day I was told by Mum that I had won 75 rupees. I had drawn a horse called Breinz which came third in the English Derby. With the money I bought a beautiful toy

Below:
The horse trainer, Tod Hewitt, (marked x) who ruined my boyish dreams.

jockey on a horse made by Britains. It was five inches high and the jockey wore the racing colours of Lord Derby, black with a white sash.

At the age of seven, my ambition was to become a jockey. My hopes were dashed by our Australian horse trainer, Tod Hewitt. He was a friend of the family, whose swearing used to horrify my mother and Gran. 'You'll be too bloody big for a jockey,' he said. I said if I couldn't be a jockey, I would be a train driver. He told me I would be too small for a train driver!

Then came a thrilling occasion for me – a Bristol fighter flew low over Poona and landed at Poona racecourse. We all ran to see it. To me, as a small boy, it was like an apparition. It was so big and beautiful. The pilot let me sit in the cockpit – it was Heaven! From then on, I didn't want to be a jockey, I wanted to be a pilot. That wish stayed with me until the day we returned to England. So impressed with the plane was Uncle Hughie that he made a model of it, exact down to the last minute detail. I took it on the school

Right:
Heavens! First in class – me!

Convent of Jesus and Mary

High School, Primary Division

REPORT

Standard I.
Of Master Terence Milligan
During Last Term 1927
Conduct Good. Application Much better
Attendance Good.

PROGRESS IN CLASS

		MARKS OBTAINED 70	MARKS OBTAINABLE 100	REMARKS
CATECHISM & SACRED HISTORY				
English	Reading	100	100	
	Recitation	100	100	
	Dictation	86	100	Order of merit.
	Grammar	34	50	
	Composition	42	50	
Class Subject	Geography	46	100	1st. among 17. pupils.
	History	—		
	Writing	30	100	Promoted.
	Nature Study	40	100	
	French	—	100	
	Arithmetic	90	100	
	Geometry	—	—	
Hand	Drawing	35	100	
	Needle work	40	100	
	Music	—		
	Total	643	1000	

N.B.—A pupil, who has obtained ⅔ of the maximum marks, is doing well in the class; if she obtains less than ⅓ she is doing badly.

Poona. January 1928 School re-opens

N. Mary Superioress.

Anand Press.-Anand.

bus, attached it to a stick and held it out the window to make the propellor revolve. Unfortunately, it fell off.

I taught myself to play the ukulele and one evening found myself sitting with Aunty Eileen outdoors in cane chairs, while Sergeant Kidd of the Ulster Rifles knelt before her. He was singing Irving Berlin's waltz 'I'll Be Loving You Always' (how many ways was that?) and I was enthusiastically accompanying him on the uke. He stopped singing and said, 'It's too high for me, kid. Can you play it lower down?'

Above:

Cowboys! In this photo my mother appears to be pregnant with my brother, Desmond.

I didn't know how to, so he changed into a lower key. If ever someone wanted me to bugger off, it was him.

At Christmas, the Convent put on a nativity play. Nuns are notoriously slow at scene changes and to fill in the time they dressed me up in a clown's costume, blacked up my face, giving me big white lips, and pushed me out in front of the curtain to entertain. One of the few benefits of political correctness is that today's children will not be subjected to such an ordeal. All I could think of doing was to roll my eyes, open and close my thick white lips and jump up and down. That brought gales of laughter. At last came the final scene of the nativity. Oh, dear – the nuns didn't want me to appear as a clown in this scene. Something in my small heart told me this was wrong, so I waited for the scene to be set and then I suddenly appeared in the middle of the archangels! The audience loved it and burst into a round of applause. It would be a long time before I would enjoy that sort of reception again, but it lingered long in my infant head.

For coming first in class, I had to collect a prize on award day. My mum was very proud as I stepped forward to receive my prize – a copy of *Alice in Wonderland*. That evening, the whole family went to the circus at

Below:

Me with Aunty Eileen, friends and Topi, Poona, 1924.

Ganishkind. I watched as a man was fired from a cannon, motorcyclists rode through hoops of fire on the wall of death – and then there were the lions. The tamer wore a leopard-skin shirt, the lions sat on blocks and obeyed his every command, now and then lashing the air with a paw. They, too, jumped through hoops of flame and one lion put his paws on the trainer's shoulders and licked his face.

Finally, there was an Italian trio of acrobats, all dressed in white tights. They were called 'The Angelinas' and I was in awe as they just seemed to float in the air, almost missing the trapeze. And the woman had a big bum.

The Governor General's Annual Parade took place at the Polo Ground. Under the blazing Indian sun, regiments of infantry, lancers and gunners filed past in grand array. First came the Ulster Rifles in blinding-white starched uniforms, black buttons and green forage caps, preceded by a bugle band playing the American Civil War song 'As We Were Marching To Georgia'. The silver bugles flashed in the sun.

The Cheshire Regiment marched

Above:
Leo again in cowboy gear ...

with his baton. Next came a battalion of the Rajputana Rifles in scarlet jackets and the Welsh Fusiliers, in starched white. They were led by a white-horned goat with gold collar and chain.

Then came the highly polished 18-pounder guns of the Royal Artillery, each pulled by six, equally polished, black horses. The entire team of gunners were in best-dress Artillery Blues. The brass of the guns gleamed like gold.

Overhead flew a squadron of Bristol Bulldogs in V formation. Below them rode the cream of the Indian Army – the Bengal lancers! They all rode brown horses which shone so much they looked as though they had been varnished. Their riders were in blue jackets, black trousers with a blue stripe, blue puggrees with red inset and spurs

Right:

... along with Hughie prior to a 1928 hunting trip.

past in starched stiff khaki, their polished brass buttons bouncing in the sunlight. Then came the bagpipes of the 2/4 Gurkhas (the Scots have got a lot to answer for), their drum major performing wonderful twirling tricks

— Rangoon Times —
— 1926 —

**BUCKING PONY
DEFEATED
LOCAL RIDER'S SUCCESS**

There is at least one rider in Rangoon who must feel proud of his powers as an equestrian. He is R.Q.M.S. Milligan of the Port Defence. The reason for his pride is that he rode a real bucking pony successfully at the Rodeo Show on Saturday night. There was a large gathering present who enjoyed the various acts presented for their delectation. The Cossack Riders, of course, took pride of place for nothing like their act has ever before been seen in Rangoon. It was a revelation of the art of trick-riding and very enjoyable at that. After numerous acts had been performed and appreciated the real thrills began. The Manager announced that buck-riding would commence and that there were a couple of local competitors taking part. Excitement ran high. A bay horse was led into the ring. He looked a quiet animal and gave no trouble when being saddled. Mr. Wright mounted the animal but did not stay on. At the second buck he became acquainted with the hardness of the turf which covers that portion of the eastern lung of the city. He was cheered for his attempt, and he fully deserved the applause. Then there walked into the ring Milligan, carrying his own saddle. "Theda Bara" was brought out. She was a grey animal, docile in appearance but with a spirit which refused to be curbed by bit or bridle. The saddle was adjusted. Milligan jumped on Thedabara, and the manner in which she began to buck made one nervous as to what was going to result. But Milligan was game. He stuck on "like stick-phast," and amid cries of encouragement from the cowboys and the plaudits of the spectators he rode the animal the regulation distance. The management announced that he had won the prize of Rs. 100 and he was given a rousing reception. Immediately he issued a challenge to ride "White Lightning," an animal which has, according to his owner, withstood all attempts at riding for eleven years.

When "White Lightning" was led out on Saturday night she showed she was the possessor of a fiery temper. It was with the greatest difficulty she was saddled. She snorted and puffed and there was a wicked gleam in her eye. A young man called Jones got on her but before he could commence his journey he was hurled through the air on to the not too kindly bosom of mother earth. It will be a remarkable act for Milligan if he conquers her.

There was one act on the part of some rowdy spectators on Saturday night which did not meet with approval. Just after Milligan had conquered Theda Bara some young men shouted a few insulting remarks to the manager who was in the ring. This sort of behaviour does not add to the reputation of Rangoon and the sooner it is stopped the better.

The proprietors of the Rodeo informed us that Theda Bara is one of their fastest bucking mares. R.Q.M.S. Milligan rode his own saddle and was provided by the show authorities with cowboy boots and chaps. The proprietor, Mr Jack Burroughs, and his cowboys and cowgirls, are genuinely delighted with the Britisher's triumph, and Mr. Milligan in return speaks highly of the fair show given him by the Westerners.

The army man's next venture will be on Tuesday, when he will possibly ride the unbeaten White Lightning, as the names of all the horses are to be put in a net and drawn for.

sparkling on their black, polished riding boots. They went by at the trot, the horses' bits jangling on their teeth.

So it went on, unit after unit, ending up with a display of tent pegging by Pathan horsemen.

What I was experiencing was the end of the Empire.

By now I was having repeated bouts of fever and becoming delirious. The fever had the strange effect of making me feel as if my hands and feet were huge. I was dosed with quinine which gave me a ringing in my ears. At times I was really quite ill. My mother must have been beside herself with worry and it couldn't have helped that my father was so far away, although he was home on leave from time to time.

In May, Leo was promoted to acting rank Regimental Sergeant Major. He was also still performing, appearing in cabaret the the Vienna Café in Rangoon. Furthermore, he was about to become a father again. My mother was pregnant.

Later that year, my mother

Left:
Press cutting of my father's rodeo triumph in Rangoon.

Below:
Florence, Desmond and Grandma in the garden at 5 Climo Road.

Above:
Lake Karikiwasla, 1928. Me in foreground, Mum, Aunty Eileen and her fanny further out.

Right:
On the trip to the lake I was befriended by a dog. I'm the one on the right.

and I journeyed by rail to Calcutta. It was an overnight journey and, being Europeans, we travelled first class. We had our own berth on the train and I slept in the upper bunk. When the train stopped at occasional stations I remember the cries of the vendors: 'Dood, gurama dood!' (Milk, hot milk!); 'Gurama pani!' (Hot water!); 'Naringi, cayler!' (Oranges, bananas!). Right above my bunk was a red chain which disappeared into a pipe at either end. So what did I do? I pulled it. The train came grinding to a halt. Mother asked me if I had pulled the chain. I said, of course I had! An Anglo-Indian guard came bustling down the line. He knocked at the door of our berth

and asked, with that wonderful Indian accent, 'Excuse me, madam, but anybody in this cabin pulling the emergency?'

My mother gave profuse apologies.

'I'm so sorry. My little boy pulled it. I'm so sorry.'

'Think nothing of it, madam,' he said. Well, I didn't think much of it either. In the morning, we washed with hot water in the polished steel basins. We steamed into Calcutta with its smells, monkeys, sacred cows and poverty.

Taking a gahari to the docks we boarded a ship of the Bibby Line. Our final destination was Rangoon where we were to join my father and settle into a house on stilts in 15 Godwin Road.

On 5 December my mother gave birth to my brother, Desmond Patrick.

1926

When Desmond was at the crawling stage, my father discovered a deadly, small snake called a Krite slithering close to him. He killed it with a broom. It could have been a disaster if little Desmond had reached for the snake.

Desmond was, however, used to strange things creeping towards him.

Top left:

Photo of my father which he sent to me on my birthday in 1929.

Above:

The letter which accompanied the photo.

Right:

Father gave me a gunbelt for my birthday and I was forced to dress up as a cowboy.

My father and I would make him laugh by crawling towards him singing 'Doodles and Bums, Doodles and Bums.' It makes the snake incident seem quite tame.

When he wasn't crawling around the floor talking rubbish, my father found time to win a hundred rupees, by successfully riding a bucking bronco in a visiting American rodeo show. He dressed, of course, as a cowboy. I was there and witnessed the whole thing. I walked among the audience selling programmes with a phoney American accent.

In October, my mother received a telegram from Uncle Hughie saying that Grandma had threatened to blow her brains out (supposing she missed?) because Eileen had been having an affair with some bastard called McIntire. Someone had to be there, so Florence booked a trip to

Left:
A halt on the way to the DAK bungalow in Patas, 1928. With us came the ayah and Thumby.

Below:
A gahari similar to the one which once brought my father home dead drunk.

India with Desmond and me. Surprise! we sailed on the SS *Erinpura*, the same ship we had been shipwrecked on in the Red Sea in 1919.

1927

My father remained in Rangoon and was sent on various courses by the army, passed his First Class Certificate of Education, and appeared in concert at the University Boat Club in Rangoon.

1928

Leo attended a gunnery instruction course in Kakul, India, in September, after which he put on a show called the Kakulunatics. ('Doodles and Bums, Doodles and Bums.') Following the course, he was

Above:
My father and a false
moustache, Rangoon, 1928.

given leave and he came to visit us in Poona. I remember we all picnicked at Lake Karikiwasla, just outside Poona.

It wasn't long before Leo persuaded Hughie to get into cowboy gear, possibly to get him in the mood for the next Kettleband and Milligan huntin', shootin' and fishin' trip. We were driven to Patas in an army truck.

During the stay at the DAK bungalow, my father took me out hunting. Luckily, we didn't come across any game, so we didn't have to shoot anything, though I was perfectly willing to have a go. (Oh, how I have changed!)

I awoke one night at the bungalow with the bright moonlight streaming through the bars on my window. I looked outside and there, large as life, was a tiger! I didn't wake my father as he would immediately have wanted to shoot it. In the morning, I recounted the incident to him. 'Why didn't you tell me, son? I would have shot it!'

By December, my father's leave was up and we all started the long train journey across India towards Burma. All day I watched the telegraph wires going from one post to the next. I liked it when the sound of the wheels changed tone over a long bridge. Flashing past us were the ancient, timeless peasants, working their fields, using wooden ploughs drawn by bullocks. I think they

still are – still
ploughing,
still working,
still timeless
and ancient, still flashing.

Calcutta! Then by ship across the Bay of Bengal to Rangoon and 15 Godwin Road where my cowboy father posed with a pencilled moustache!

1929

In April, my father must have been away from home again, because he sent me a letter on my birthday along with a photograph of him dressed as – guess what – a cowboy. When he got back, he gave me a gunbelt as a present and I then had to dress up as a cowboy, too.

One day Dad came home around noon in a gahari (a kind of horse-drawn

taxi), dead drunk. It was the one and only time I saw him in that state. My mother pounced on him, shrieking at him. She had the tongue of a viper. God knows where she got it. She kept on at him non-stop until he fell asleep on his bed.

We moved from 15 Godwin Road

to Brigade House in Lewis Road. It was a lovely, large, airy home in the grounds

Left:
Brigade House, Rangoon.

Below:
Desmond on the verandah at Brigade House.

Top Left:

Tourists! Visiting a temple in Burma…

Top Right:

…and on a bridge.

of the III Field Brigade Compound, the cantonment. At first there was no electricity in the house but soon two Chinese contractors started the installation. The unending tap-tap-tap of their hammers drove Leo mad and he threw both of them, and their ladders, out. Finally, after having been thrown out a few times, they completed the job – we had three-speed overhead fans!

In the Brigade grounds was a drill hall and a bar with billiards and a wind-up console gramophone. It was there that I played my first jazz record, Fats Waller playing 'I'll Be Glad When You're Dead You Rascal You', and my first crooner, Morton Downey singing 'Weary River'. I also made my first girl contact there – Vera Watson. She, her mother, Ruth, and Sergeant Watson lived in the other half of Brigade House.

My father gave Desmond and me a couple of old muskets and we would wander around pretending to shoot . . . birds, dogs, cats, tigers and people. It was harmless fun, but what if he had given us real rifles?

1930

In January, I was enrolled at St Paul's High School, run by the Brothers De La Salle. Brother John was the senior of the school. I remember when I went to his office he would stink of brandy. The other pupils were mostly Burmese boys and I was put in a class with an English-

speaking Burmese teacher. His nickname was 'Porky' and he was a

Sergeant in the 14th Machine Gun Company attached to III Field Brigade.

I joined the 14th Machine Gun Company as a cadet and, by the time I was 12, I could dismantle a Vickers 303 machine gun and re-assemble it. There was a rifle range in the grounds and we would often have practice shoots. I was a pretty good shot.

In March, Leo gave a concert in Rangoon but, more exciting than that, slight earth tremors were felt. There were more to come.

Above:
Leo danced and sang 'Roll On You Mississippi, Roll On' in a concert for the blind, December 1929

Left:
Me and Desmond tired out with pretend shooting.

Right:
Me and Desmond looking
for a pretend shoot.

Below:
Entire 14th Machine Gun
Company.

Leo received a telegram in October telling him of Elizabeth Milligan's death in Poplar. She was 77. He was very distressed and took us all to the pictures (silent in those days). That night I heard him crying in bed. We had to hang the pillow out to dry.

Great excitement! In November we were given free tickets to see Rudolph Valentino in *The Sheikh*. The film would stop five times to change reels. Those were the days. December brought a terrible earthquake to Rangoon. I was upstairs having a cold bath. The door started to rattle and I said, 'Koowan hai?' (Who's there?).

Then I heard the noise of hundreds of crows cawing and the medicine bottles on the shelf fell over. I grabbed a towel. By now the whole house was shaking. I leapt down the stairs three

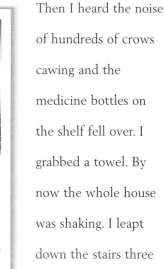

at a time and ran into the garden where my father was holding my brother with my mother, all staring at the house.

None of us spoke, but I remember the deafening cawing of the crows, disturbed from their nests. 'Better wait a while in case there's another one,' said Dad. We waited, there wasn't.

Yet more excitement! My mother and father went to the cinema to see their first <u>sound</u> film called *Rio Rita* with John Bowles and Bebe Daniels. She was later to appear on the radio in *Life With The Lyons*. I listened to my father describe the film – 'You could hear everything, the pistol shots, the singing, the talking.' So I went to see it. I still remember the songs: 'Rio Rita, life is sweeter, Rita, when you are near.' And the Texas Rangers' song; 'We're all

pals together, we're all pals forever.'

For some reason my father was summoned for money owing to Mesquite and Company. The reason was he hadn't paid it. All his life he was hopeless with money. The night before his court appearance, he rehearsed his defence. 'I ask you, was it worth a court case for such a trivial sum? As soon as I got the summons, I ordered my bank to pay it forthwith. At this moment in time, it must be in the post.' What a bloody liar! He didn't have a bank. Somehow, he managed to get himself

Above:
Leo mastering a tractor.

Below:
Press report of the earthquake.

Right:
My first suit – pale blue!

EARTHQUAKE.
DISASTER IN BURMA.
Hundreds of Lives Lost.
PANIC AT RANGOON.

CALCUTTA, May 6.
It is feared that over 500 people are dead in Pegu, in Burma, as the result of an earthquake last night, followed by fire and flood waters from the rivers Pegu and Sittang.

Rail and telegraph communications are cut off, but medical aid is being rushed to the scene of the disaster by road.

Fifty people were killed and over 200 injured in Rangoon, where the shocks were the worst in living memory.

Many buildings at Rangoon, including the High Court and Catholic Cathedral, have been severely damaged.

Most of the casualties occurred in a Mosque and a five-story building, which collapsed, burying all the occupants.

The population fled panic-stricken from houses, and spent the remainder of the night in parks and other open spaces.

The fire brigade laboured all night to rescue the trapped victims.

The town has been plunged into darkness, owing to the breaking of electric cables.

off on the promise that he would pay the debt. He drew the money out of his wallet (I swear that moths flew out of it) and handed it to the Mesquite and Company solicitor. He had borrowed the cash from an Indian money lender. He arrived home gloating, 'I showed 'em. I gave 'em what for.' Most of all, what he gave 'em was the money.

By now I had gathered a small army of boys around me. We paraded for Lord Wellington whose car was due to pass by our house. Despite our parade, he didn't pass by that day. Fuck him!

I contracted a terribly high fever, my temperature soaring to 105° – dangerously high, but only for me. My parents spent hours dousing me with cold water. I was so ill, I shit the bed. A doctor attended me twice a day. Eventually the fever subsided, but I had lost a stone in weight. To put it back on they gave me Sanatogen!

1931

In February, Leo was granted one year's leave in England. We went by ship to Calcutta, then the long train journey to

Far Left:
Me and my army awaiting the passing of Lord Wellington.

Above :
My army in battle.

Below:

Stopping them with a machine gun aimed low. Were they Japanese?

Far Right:

My bed was moved out onto the verandah to keep me cool during my worst fever.

Poona where we stayed with the Kettlebands.

On 7 March we took the *Deccan Queen* from Poona to Bombay where we embarked on the SS *Kaiser I Hind*, known for its speed as the greyhound of the fleet. On the main deck were what had been mountings for guns during World War I. We were second class passengers, but really had all the luxury of first class.

As we travelled through the Med, a canvas swimming pool was erected on the deck. In it I learnt to swim, and my brother learnt to drown. A rope hung above the pool. We would swing across from one side to the other. Alas, half way across, Desmond lost his hold, fell in the water and started to drown. He would have done just that but for the efforts of a little girl who said to my father in a funny little voice, 'He's fallen in the water!'

That would become one of the catch phrases in *The Goon Show.*

We docked at Tilbury and went by train to Waterloo followed by taxi to the Union Jack Club where we stayed temporarily until we moved to Rosenthal Road in Catford. We had the top floor – part attic and bedrooms. In the attic was a bed for our parents.

Their room also had a gas stove and a sink. For the first time in her life, my mother had to cook for us.

Desmond and I spent the days playing with toy soldiers that we bought at the rate of one penny per soldier from Woolworths. Our Aunty Cathleen, Dad's sister, lent us a gramophone with some records including

Above:
The Greyhound of the Fleet.

Left:
Posing with other passengers in Aden, a shit-strewn hell hole.

Top:

Mum, Aunt Nance, me and Desmond on the front porch in Sittingbourne. I'm wearing the cap of Brownhill Road School, Catford.

'The William Tell Overture', the finale of which we played as the climax to our battles.

We visited Aunt Nance in Sittingbourne who had had charge of me as an infant. She was delighted that I wasn't screaming any more.

On one embarrassing occasion, my father caught me wanking. He said, 'Stop that! Do you want all your children to be thin?' Well, I was so thin that he must have spent all his spare time doing it.

Our landlord, a sailor in World War I, lived in the basement. He asked me what I was going to do. Apart from wanking, I really didn't know.

Uncle Alf, Cathleen's husband, had a car and drove us to see the speedway riding at Crystal Palace. The Crystal Palace was a marvel to me, built mostly from glass. Years later, from my bedroom in Riseldene Road in Brockley, I would see it burning. My father saw the flames and said, 'Navaho!'

In Catford was the Queen's Cinema. Dad would lend me money (Lend me money? It was only three-pence to get in!) for me and Desmond to go. We liked cowboy films (why?) with Tom Mix and Hoot Gibson. In the interval, the commissionaire would walk up and down the aisle spraying scent. It never happened in India.

My father took me to the Rotunda in Woolwich. To his surprise, the attendant was an old soldier friend. They stood and chewed the fat while I went round looking at a wondrous collection of guns. One was an astounding Chinese dragon gun captured during the Boxer rebellion when an overpowering force of British, American and French attacked a hopelessly under-equipped Chinese Army. Let's hope the present-day Chinese Army doesn't remember.

We also went to the British Museum where we saw the stunning ancient gates of Khorsabad in Assyria. I was filled with wonder at that, and the Elgin Marbles. I marvelled at the detail of a horse's head. Everywhere I was surrounded by statues and objects of the ancient world. I think it was the beginning of my interest in archaeology – I've been collecting ever since.

One day my Uncle Alf drove us down to Brighton, then still a small seaside town. I was overpowered by the sheer brilliance of the Inigo Jones Pavillion. Each room was fascinating.

Top Left:
Some of the performers at yet another function in Rangoon, 1932.

'This was built by the Prince Regent,' said Dad. 'Oh, all by himself?' asked Desmond. Naturally, we went on the pier, bought ice creams and looked at 'What The Butler Saw'. To me, who had seen Aunty Eileen's fanny, the Butler hadn't seen that much.

Back in London we saw the Tower and the Crown Jewels. How much were they worth? Desmond valued them at £3. 'Much more than that,' said Dad. 'Okay, £4,' said Desmond. We fed the ravens. 'If ever the ravens disappear from the Tower, the Empire will fall.' Oh, dear, I thought. Could those ravens be relied upon? One man with a shotgun could knock them all off! Before the war, why hadn't the Kaiser sent a German to shoot them all and win World War I?

Buckingham Palace. We waited all day for the King and Queen to appear

Below:
Entire III Brigade, Royal Artillery, Burma.

Left:
Desmond, immature cowboy about to start school, Rangoon 1932.

Above:
A snake charmer plying his trade. They said the fangs had been removed. It didn't look like it to me!

on the balcony. My uninformed father kept saying, 'Any minute now they'll come out, you'll see.' We waited and waited, but we didn't see. So we watched the guards marching back and forth only to then watch them march forth and back.

1932

In February we returned to Burma, boarding the SS *Letetia* in Liverpool,

bound for Bombay. We stopped at Gibraltar, Marseilles, Suez , Port Saïd and Aden. We went ashore at Malta, where we saw the Black Gates in the Cathedral. I was told the name derived from the time of Napoleon. The gates were solid silver and were painted black in case some of his soldiers looted them. They were only given one coat, so it must have been Dulux.

At Suez, merchants pulled their boats alongside and bartered goods using a basket on a rope. We didn't go ashore in Aden because of the heat. I didn't understand. It was just as hot on the ship! Ah, but we did have a canvas swimming pool and iced lemonade.

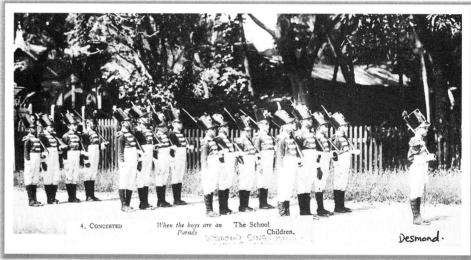

4. CONCERTED   *When the boys are on*   The School
                Parade   Children.

Desmond.

On the evening of the 27th, there was a concert on board ship. Mum and Dad, as old professionals, wowed them. Des and I did a shadow show. Behind a sheet lit from the back, we appeared to be operating on a body from which we removed things like a frying pan, a telephone, a pair of pliers, a saw, and so on. Finally we brought out a baby, the sheet was dropped and we were holding a real live baby which we had borrowed from a lady passenger. The trouble was, all through the act the baby was crying! Desmond, the little show-off, also sang – 'When The Guards Are On Parade'.

There was a stopover at Poona. Grandma and Eileen and her fanny were still there. Hughie had enlisted in the West Kents Band.

Back in Rangoon in March, Desmond started school at The Convent Of The Good Shepherd, but first had to be photographed as a cowboy. I continued my schooling at St Paul's High School. I used to cycle to school and would stop off to have a glass of sugar cane juice that was squeezed from the canes by the road vendor. Once there was also a Burmese artist at work, drawing pictures of people screwing. I stayed long enough to take it in.

Left:
Desmond leads an army with nowhere to go.

Above:
R.S.M. Leo Milligan, the moment he had taken off his cowboy kit.

Top Right:
Me preparing for a hot summer.

I got to know an Anglo-Indian called Murray who worked in a charity shop in Rangoon. He thought it would be a good idea for me to borrow my father's cowboy outfit and appear behind the charity sales counter. I enjoyed it so much I skipped school for three weeks. When my father found out, he took me in the back room and thrashed me with a cane – or so everyone thought. He swished the cane about a lot, but he never hit me. He did it to satisfy my bloody mother.

Every evening after school I would have a cold bath, put on a sparkling white shirt and creased trousers and, for some unknown reason, a sleeveless cardigan. Then I would walk to The Firs to see my friend, Dick Latimer. His mother had married for a second time to a sarcastic Scotsman called Anderson. I'm not sure what he did, but whatever it was, he did it. We would leave the house when Mr Anderson gave Mrs Anderson her daily enema.

At Christmas, my father arranged for the male children to put on a show. All the boys were dressed in uniform with Desmond as Captain. They sang 'When The Guards Are On Parade' – Desmond's party piece – and it went down a storm with the boys marching and counter-marching, all crashing into each other.

1933

It was early in the New Year when my

backwards! The doctor arrived in an ambulance and gave Dad a shot of morphine. Immediately

father came staggering back from the Battery Office. Was he ill, or did he just want the day off? No, he had stones in the kidneys and was soon in bed moaning with pain. I borrowed the Brigade bike and rode like fury to the cantonment hospital. I was rushing downhill to a crossroads where the trams crossed. I tried to brake, but there weren't any. I caught my breath as I raced across the cross-roads. Thank God that no trams were passing. I was told later that you could brake by pedalling

the pain stopped. He looked at us through tranquillised eyes and said, 'Oh, you all look like angels.' How he could have thought someone as acne-ridden as me was an angel . . .

One of our ayahs was Winnie Ma. She was plump and shapely and would bathe under an outside shower wearing a thin gown. When it was wet, we could see it all. She tried to shoo us away, but we stuck it out, as most of her did. Lots of innocent fun in Rangoon.

Part II orders on 8 April brought a

Top Left:
Mother playing tennis with Wimbledon a million miles away.

Above:
A farewell photograph
outside Brigade House.

shock for my father. The post of R.S.M. was abolished as from 1 April. He had been expecting this since February. To try to reverse this decision, he dictated a pathetic letter to the Commanding Officer, Major Perrot, signed by all the NCOs. It failed. He must have been very naive. I think he dreaded the thought of leaving the army after all those years. He must have thought it would go on forever. It did, but he didn't. He had no idea, what kind of job he should look for in civvy street. Something to do with horses, maybe? There aren't many openings for a retired cowboy.

I became quite proficient on the billiards table at the Brigade Club. My biggest break was 43. A bigger break was my right arm when I fell whilst trying to walk round a first-floor ledge outside the house. I was annoyed. It was the arm I used to wank with.

Soon we were on our way back to the UK. Once again there was the ship to Calcutta and the train to Poona. Grandma and Eileen and her fanny – all three greeted us at the station. We stayed in Poona for a couple of weeks. I spent the days swimming, swimming, wanking and swimming. On 6 May we embarked on the SS *Rajputana* at

Bombay. I had a very fine outside cabin with a porthole. I watched Bombay in the sunset as we pulled away from the shore. One thing I didn't see was a member of the crew being cut in half by a recoiling wire hawser. Blast!

These days my father was bald and wore a terrible wig which looked like a dead cat nailed to his head. Alas, during a windy day aboard ship, it blew off. He retrieved it with one hand whilst covering his bald head with the other. A similar incident had occurred in Rangoon when he gave Desmond and me pistols loaded with blank cartridges. He was the target, running from rock to rock, firing blanks back at us. But, oh, dear, oh, dear, the kite hawks of Rangoon were constantly being shot at and, the moment he fired his blanks back at us, a kite hawk dived down on him and arose with his wig in its claws. That night he wrote to England with a clawed head to order a new wig. In the meantime, he would wear his topi hat non-stop, even when he was indoors. He even wore it at dinner so the servants never knew.

In due course the replacement wig arrived and it was every bit as terrible as the first one. From then on he stuck it on with powerful glue. He must have run out of glue on the *Rajputana*.

We went ashore at Malta where my father tried to order *trois cafés au lait*. The waiter didn't understand, he only

Below:

SS Rajputana.

P. & O. S.S. RAJPUTANA, 16,600 TONS GROSS.
India Mail and Passenger Service.

Above:

My mother in an evening gown, part of the lifestyle we were leaving behind.

spoke Maltese, so Dad ordered 'three coffees with milk.' The waiter brought us three boiled eggs. To save face, we ate them anyway.

On 16 May there was a concert on board. Marie Prescott performed the opening number with Marie Hag. Marie Prescott I had an eye on and she had an eye on me. I was 15, she was 16, beating me by a year. Leo did a violent buck-and-wing step dance. I watched his wig. Would it stand up to this treatment? He later said it had been a near thing. Oh, the courage of the man.

Back to Marie Prescott. She and I were in a returning soldier's cabin. She suddenly said, 'Will you kiss me?' Well, I didn't know about French kissing, or fucking, or fighting come to that. Our lips touched. She immediately said, 'Oh, why don't you kiss me like in the cinema?' I took a deep breath and there was a knock at the door. Marie hid in the toilet. Why? The door was opened, in walked a fifty-five-year-old harridan. Her eyes swept the cabin. 'I've heard,' she threatened, 'there's a girl in here!' The soldier and I were dumbstruck. The Harridan said, 'I'm going to tell the Captain about this!' 'This'? What was 'this'? Me, we all three, 'this'??? To avoid the Captain, Miss Prescott left. It was my last chance. Never mind, I would have a good wank that night after dinner.

GROWING FURTHER UP IN ENGLAND

1933

On 26 May we docked at Tilbury and travelled to London where we stayed at the Union Jack club before moving to 22 Gabriel Street in Honor Vale Park. There we rented part of the house.

The landlady was a 65-year-old harridan, Mrs Windust – 'All 'angers-on to be shot off.' The parlour was sacred, we were only admitted on Sunday. The piano – 'We 'ave it tuned regularly' – keys were covered with a cloth. Could my mother play it? 'Yes, but I'll 'ave to unlock it first.' When my mother eventually played it, Mrs Windust was struck dumb. 'Oh,' she said. 'I've never heard it played before. My aunty bought it for me as a wedding present!'

The first week there, Leo went to the tailors in Catford to buy a Barney Built suit. Must look good to get a job. It was, for its day, a very good suit – next

Leo and family aboard the
Rajputana with wig in place.

day, not so good. To go with it, he bought a black homburg hat and grey kid gloves. He would wear one and hold the other in his hand. Along with this went an ebony-black cane with a silver boss. Thus attired he would take a 74 tram to Catford and walk up and down the main road. 'You never know who you'll meet,' he said. He didn't meet anybody and came back on a 74 tram.

Mum had to start cooking again. We had 'down-market meals' – pigs trotters, tripe and onions, oxtail soup, cod's roe, sweetbreads and bread and butter pudding. Then there was custard, just custard. We never went hungry.

Above Left:
Leo and Florence, he throwing caution to the wind with hat off.

Above:
Desmond on deck.

Above:
Outside a café in Malta.

From June until Christmas, I attended Woolwich and Greenwich Day Continuation School. God knows why. I also went to evening classes at Kilmore Road and Dad paid for me to have private lessons in mathematics. I thought that this would help me pass the entrance exam to become a pilot in the RAF.

1934

It didn't. I sat the exam in a building in Kingsway. I failed miserably. In early January, I got a job at Stones Engineering.

I was a clerk to a dying bookkeeper. I was bloody hopeless.

Around this time I also met my first girlfriend. Her name was Nina Hall. She had magnificent boobs. I would like to have screwed her, but I was too shy. Eventually, someone else did.

It was in her flat that I heard my first Bing Crosby record and I was hooked on him. I soon realised that I could imitate Bing very well. For a while I sang with a very good band, The New Era Rhythm Boys. I won a crooning contest at the Lady Florence Institute. All this crooning came before the guitar period in popular music and I was in my element. I came second in a talent contest at Lewisham Hippodrome.

At Stones I was transferred to testing fuse boxes. I had to use one positive and

one negative prod. I would regularly give myself powerful electric shocks, so, before I killed myself, they transferred me again to the machine room. There I was taught how to operate a Miller cutting machine. A steel rod an eighth of an inch thick would run in from the right. I would feed it left where a sharp steel tool would peel half of it, hammer this, cut it off and drop it in a bin.

I worked very hard as I was paid by the number of these things I produced. The job ended when, whilst bending down, my hair was caught in the revolving rod, ripping out a clump and giving me a bald patch. For this I was told, 'Get your cards!' – I was sacked. For months I had to wear a cap 24 hours a day.

In May, Leo applied for a job with Associated Press in Farringdon Street. He was accepted on a starvation wage. I was earning ten shillings a night doing gigs. At this time I also learned to play the bass and worked with lots of bands. To transport the bass around town, you had to put it in the front of the tram along with the driver and there was always the same boring joke, 'Can you get it under your chin?' Same old English standard humour.

I soon had another job as a van boy delivering confectionery and sweets. I had access to whatever I wanted. I ate so

Left:
22 Gabriel Street, where the prisoners were held.

Above:
Leo inside Barney Built suit assisted by my mother.

many Bassett's Liquorice Allsorts that I had the shits for a week. Next I was a workhand in the Chislehurst Laundry. There were three men, me, and one hundred randy women. They would squeeze a wet pocket handkerchief into the shape of a man's willy and say to me, 'Is yours like this?' I didn't dare tell them that mine was four times that size through wanking. Some of those laundry girls were luscious but I was too bloody shy to date any of them – oh, the lost chances! I left when my leaky gum-boots let in water and caused me to get World War I trench foot.

I was still seeing Nina Hall and not doing it to her. At the time of Mosley, she started wearing a black shirt. I wondered why Jews kept shouting 'Fascist' at us in the street. What was a Fascist? I'll tell you, *she* was.

Not satisfied with playing double bass, I wanted an instrument to make a bigger noise. A trumpet, that's what I needed.

1935

After work I would go to London Bridge station. I remember sitting in a crowded 3rd-class carriage when a very pretty girl came in. I got up to give her my seat. I didn't know that she had seen me on the train previously. She said, 'No, thank you. I'll just sit on your lap.' That was the start of my first serious affair. Her name was Lily Dunford and we started going steady.

She was not classically beautiful, but attractive with lovely legs, bum and boobs. They were all my size! We went to dances and then back to the porch of 43 Revlon Road, Brockley, and snogged. Oh, the curse of erections that stick out of your trousers. I had to wear a jockstrap to contain it. It didn't work. It just got very hot. Lily desperately wanted me to marry her, but I was woolly headed enough to think that we could go on as we were forever.

Lily, I think, planned this . . . It was Whit Monday. She asked me round to her house. Her mother was away and for the first time we had access to a bed. I realised that under her loose housecoat, she was naked. It was a trap and I fell for it! I had no idea where a vagina was; I thought it was in the front amid the pubic hairs. Eventually I found it, I also found that she was a virgin. I didn't know that, she told me later. I made a meal of it. I didn't want to orgasm inside her, so I withdrew with a scream and crossed eyes!

She lent (gave) me money for my first trumpet. It was four pounds ten shillings. It was a piece of crap. I practised on it with a sock in the bell. Finally I mastered it and started playing

Above:
Reference from the Greenwich and Woolwich Day Continuation School.

Right:
Nina Hall, who I didn't do it to.

first trumpet with a weekend gig band. By now Lily had gone off me. It hurt me terribly; I went on loving her.

As the year progressed I started weight training at the Ladywell Recreation Grounds. A group of us weightlifted in bathing trunks and one day a group of girls came to watch us from behind the railings. One was a stunningly pretty, blonde girl with a beautiful figure. I chatted with her – at that age I was really a pretty-looking boy. If only I had known that, I would have played my cards better. It was a whirlwind affair ending up with me seducing her in the park after dark. Her first name was Ivy but, as she is still alive, I won't give her away. She said, 'I've always had a boyfriend, ever since I was fourteen,' so I wasn't exactly a new experience.

Before long, however, she went off me, too!

I still had my trumpet, though, and was now playing lead in the New Ritz Revels. I had become a very good ad-lib soloist.

1936

On 20 January, King George V died. At the time I was working in a stationery shop in Queen Victoria Street. The firm was called S. Straker. I thought that the 'S' stood for Samuel, so when I answered the phone I'd say, 'Samuel Straker'. Someone at the shop actually was Samuel Straker and he warned me, 'Don't EVER say Samuel!' I think that

Above:
Lily (right), the girl I didn't orgasm in, with her sister.

meant we were a Jewish company and with Mosley at large, he didn't want it known.

The day of the King's death, I wore a red tie to work. Mr Elliott, the senior, said, 'You go home right now and change that tie!' By the time I got home and back again it was almost time to shut the shop – but there was still enough time for me to be fired.

From Straker's I went to work as a stockroom assistant at Keith Prowse in Bond Street. It was soul destroying. I worked under the supervision of an ape-like creature called Tom. All that kept my sanity in those days was playing evenings with the New Ritz Revels

and crooning:

> *When it's June in January, because*
>
> *I'm in love with you*
>
> *Because I'm in love with you, the snow*
>
> *is just white blossoms*
>
> *That fall from above*
>
> *Because I'm in love with you*

1937

The next job was my downfall, Spiers and Ponds Tobacco Stockroom. All day I'd wrap up a selection of tobacco and cigarettes for shops in and around London. The Senior Stockman was Mr Ripler. At the time, my £4 10/- trumpet was falling apart. How could I afford a new one? Simple, pack your overcoat pockets with fags and sell them.

I was caught by a nasty bastard, Mr Leighy. I couldn't pronounce his name

Below:

Me and next to me what I would look like if I was black.

and I didn't want to. But! I had enough for a down payment on a gold-plated Besson trumpet. I bought it from Len Stiles in Lewisham High Street.

I was fired from Spiers and Ponds and had to attend a local court. My father acted in my defence. He rehearsed his address to the court at home – 'Look at him, a young lad. His crime was his love of music. He needed the money to buy a violin and study classical music, but he was so poor he could never, you hear *never*, afford one. His only way was to pilfer stockroom goods and sell them. This has afforded him a second-hand violin which, even now, he is learning to play. Have pity on this boy because, as a result of this action, he could become a virtuoso!' What a pack of lies! With this trumpet, however, I played in yet another outfit, the Harlem Club Band.

1938

I found a reasonably paid job as a semi-skilled labourer in the dockside Woolwich Arsenal. At first, I had to be

Above:
The New Ritz Revels – I'm the Revel on the right.

Below:
Reference from my soul-destroying job with Keith Prowse.

taught how to be a semi-skilled labourer. Soon I was working on a bench making terminals for batteries and, working overtime, I earned five pounds a week. The fiver was one of those very large white notes. As usual, I gave my wages to my mother. She looked at the five pound note and said, 'What is it? Is it a cheque?' Oh, the ignorance of the poor.

At lunchtime, all the workmen would go to Carmen's Pullup, a restaurant opposite the dockyard. Serving there was a very pretty girl. Sitting in the middle of all those ugly buggers, my good looks stood out a mile. I made a date to meet her and go to the pictures to see Buck Jones in *Gun Law*. I was to meet her outside the Woolwich Odeon, so she met me outside the Woolwich Odeon – with a one-year-old baby. I watched the film, taking my turn at holding the baby. It would be the last time.

The Harlem Club Band was doing lots of gigs and earning good money. It was also a good way of meeting girls. I met up with one particularly pretty girl and, before I asked her out, I asked her if she had a baby. She said, 'No, would you like to give me one?' She took me to a country club. She said it was very expensive, but that she wanted to 'show me off'. My mother had all my money, so at the club I signed a lot of IOUs. They are still outstanding.

TELEGRAMS: STALLS, WEGOO, LONDON.
TELEPHONE: REGENT 6000 (16 LINES).

CABLES: STALLS, LONDON.
CODE: WESTERN UNION 5 LETTER EDITION.

Keith Prowse & Company Ltd

159, New Bond Street,

London 27th October, 19 38.
W. 1.

TO WHOM IT MAY CONCERN.

I would say that Terence Milligan was employed by this Company in our Wholesale Department from the 19th August, 1935, to the 29th February, 1936, during which period he discharged his duties to our entire satisfaction.

KEITH PROWSE & CO.LTD.

THE ADOLF HITLER SHOW

1939

3 September. The last minutes of peace were ticking away. Father and I were watching Mother digging our air-raid shelter. 'She's a great little woman,' said Father.

'And getting smaller all the time,' I added. Two minutes later, a man called Chamberlain, who did Prime Minister impressions, spoke on the wireless. He said, 'As from eleven o'clock we are at war with Germany.' (I loved the 'WE'.)

'War?' said Mother.

'It must have been something we said,' said Father. The people next door panicked, burnt their Post Office books and took in the washing.

One day an envelope marked O.H.M.S. fell on the mat. Father looked at his watch. 'Time for another advance,' he said, and took one pace forward. Weeks went by. Several more

My father insisted on being
photographed sitting on the
air-raid shelter.

Left:
I passed the medical; Grade 1.

Below:
Gunner Syd Carter's teeth training for war.

O.H.M.S. letters arrived, finally arriving at the rate of two a day, stamped URGENT. One Sunday, while Mother was repointing the house, Father opened one of the envelopes as a treat. In it was a cunningly worded invitation to partake in World War II, starting as seven and sixpence a week, all found.

1940

It was three months after my initial call-up. To celebrate, I hid under the bed dressed as Florence Nightingale. Next morning, I received a card asking me to attend a medical at the Yorkshire Grey in Eltham. The card said I was to report at 9.30 a.m. and I was seen promptly at 12.15. I arrived in the presence of a grey-faced, bald doctor.

'How do you feel?' he asked.

'All right,' I said.

'Do you feel fit?'

'No, I walked here.'

Grinning evilly, he wrote Grade 1 (one) in blood-red ink on my card. 'No black cap?' I asked. 'It's at the laundry,' he replied.

The die was cast. It was a proud day for the Milligan family as I was taken from the house. 'I'm too young to go,' I screamed, as

Military Policemen dragged me from my pram, clutching a dummy. At Victoria Station the R.T.O. gave me a travel warrant, a white feather and a picture of Hitler marked 'This is your enemy.' I searched every compartment, but he wasn't on the train. At 4.30 p.m., 2 June, a summer's day all mare's-tails and blue sky, we arrived at Bexhill-on-Sea where I got off. It wasn't easy. The train didn't stop there.

Apart from light military training in Bexhill, there didn't seem to be a war on at all, it was a wonderful 'shirts off' summer. Around us swept the countryside of Sussex. There were the

Above:
Making friends during a line-laying operation.

August cornfields that gave off a golden halitus, each trembling ear straining up for the sun. The Land Girls looked brown and inviting and promised an even better harvest.

I was now a trainee signaller, highly inefficient in morse, flags and helio lamps.

1941

The sole stratagem of the army in England was one of continual movement. They chose the most excruciating moments. After spending months making your billet comfortable the order came 'Prepare To Move.' I was just about to lay my new Axminster when it came. It was awful; I had to sell the piano. The moves were always highly secret and came in sealed envelopes, the contents of which usually appeared in later editions of the *Bexhill Observer*. Secrecy was impossible. Enemy agents had only to follow the trail of illegitimate births. Our first move was to a 'specially selected', muddy, disused rubbish tip at Mill Wood, two miles from Worthingholme. The signal section under Sergeant Dawson had to start the lark of laying new lines. This was simple; you went from Point A, the Observation Post (O.P.) and took the line to Point B, the Gun Position. Taking a rough bearing, we set off carrying great revolving iron drums of D.5* telephone cable. We had to cross railway lines, roads, swamps, rivers, with no more than adhesive tape. We borrowed equipment *en route* from houses; a ladder here, a pair of pliers

there, a bit of string, a few hooks, a three course lunch, etc.

At Mill Wood we lived under canvas and after a whole winter living in a tent, it was good news when we were eventually billeted in Turkey Road Girls' School. It was for us a paradise.

I took my trumpet to war. I thought I'd earn spare cash by playing Fall In, Charge, Retreat, Lights Out, etc. I put a printed card on the Battery Notice board, showing my scale of charges.

Fall In.........................1/6

Fall Out.......................1/-

Charge.........................1/9

Halt.............................£648

Retreat (Pianissimo).....4/-

Retreat (Fortissimo).....10/-

Lights Out....................3/-

Lights Out played in private.........4/-

Below:
Correct headwear for bathing during an air raid.

* I don't know what it means, either.

Above:
Apprehended by Bdr
Donaldson whilst trying
to escape.

Of course, I soon contacted the Jazz addicts. I was introduced to six-foot-two, dreamy-eyed Gunner Harry Edgington. A Londoner, he was an extraordinary man, with moral scruples that would have pleased Jesus. It was the start of a life-long friendship. Harry played the piano. Self taught. He delighted me with some tunes he had composed. He couldn't read music, and favoured two keys, F sharp and C sharp – both keys the terror of the Jazz man. Over the months, however, I'd busk tunes with him in the NAAFI. I taught him the names of various chords and he was soon playing in keys that made life easier for me. One day, with nothing but money in mind, I suggested to Harry we try and form a band. Harry grinned and looked disbelieving. 'Just the two of us?'

'We could sit far apart,' I said.

A stroke of luck. A driver, Alf Fildes, was posted to us with suspected rabies and he played the guitar! All we needed was a drummer. One meal time, as the dining hall rang to the grinding of teeth on gritty cabbages, came the sound of rhythmic beat; it was a humble gunner hammering on

Left:
Shaving al fresco.

Above:
Patriots digging drainage ditches around tents in Mill Wood.

a piece of Lease Lend bacon, trying to straighten it out for the kill. This was driver Douglas Kidgell. Would he like to be our drummer? Yes. Good. Now, where to get the drums? Gunner Nick Carter said there was a 'certain' drum kit lying fallow under the stage of the Old Town Church Hall. Captain Martin, a sort of commissioned Ned Kelly, suggested we 'requisition' the 'certain' drum kit to stop it falling into German hands. Kidgell soon got the hang of the drums and lo! we were a quartet!

After a month's practice, Captain Martin asked could we play for a dance? I told him we had a very limited repertoire. He said, 'So have I. We'll hold the dance this Saturday.' GAD! This was the big time! Saturday, the Old Town Church Hall, Bexhill! Who knows, next week, Broadway! In entertainment-starved Bexhill, the dance was a sell out. The old corrugated iron hall was packed to suffocation; there were old women, kids, officers, gunners, various wives, very much a village dance affair.

After twenty minutes we exhausted our repertoire, so we started again. Playing 'Honeysuckle Rose' forty times must be some kind of record.

D Battery Band became the centre of night life in Bexhill-on-Sea. I didn't know it at the time, but I was taking my first real steps into Show Business.

1942

Things had been going too smoothly to continue as they were. It really was time for another bout of applied chaos. It came in the shape of a sudden rush to Larkhill Artillery Camp, Salisbury, hard by Stonehenge. It was January and quite the bitterest weather I could remember. We were to practice a new speedy method of bringing a 25 pounder gun into action. From first order, through frenzied unlimbering of the gun, to the firing of the first round our time was 25 seconds – the fastest of the day.

Later in the year we were alerted for another practice shoot at

Sennybridge Camp in Wales. Burdened down with kit, I decided to hide my rifle in the rafters of a hay loft. 'That's a good idea,' said patriotic Edgington. The short of it was several others did the same. And it came to pass that after we had gone thence, there cometh a Quarter Bloke, and in the goodness of his heart, he did inspect ye hay loft, and woe, he findeth rifles and was sore distressed, whereupon he reported us to the Major who, on 14 September 1942, gave us 14 bloody days detention. I spent mine in a cell in Preston Barracks, Brighton.

In December we were given embarkation leave, a prelude to us being sent to war.

Top:
D. Battery Band. Kidgell, Fildes, Milligan and Edgington with Bdr Edser who left to be commissioned.

Above:
Crash Action winners, Larkhill.

1943

On 7 January the unit travelled by train to Liverpool where we embarked on H.M.T.L. 15, known in better days as the *SS Otranto*. By 1.10 a.m. on 8 January we had set sail. We were a mile downstream when the first bombs started to fall on the city. Ironically, a rosy glow tinged the sky. Liverpool was on fire. The lads came up on deck to see it.

Eleven days later we arrived in Algiers at dawn. The 56th Heavy Regiment disembarked and headed for the mysteriously named 'X' Camp at Cap Matifou, about 26 miles from Algiers. On 27 January the D Battery Band played at a concert in Algiers at a massive French colonial opera house where Massive French colonials once sang. Two weeks later we were on our way to the front in Tunisia and on 17 February we were dug in ready for our first action north of Bou Arada. Laying a line to our O.P., I came under fire from enemy mortars. I didn't like it, dropped the cable drum I was carrying

Above:
On embarkation leave outside my parents' house in Leatherhead where they moved when my father was commissioned in the R.A.O.C.

Right:
With Mum and Desmond, now also in the bloody army.

and made a tactical withdrawal.

We would be in action throughout the conflict in Tunisia until victory was declared in May.

In June, D Battery Band was back in concert at the 74 Medium's camp and this was followed in July by a spot in the *Stand Easy* revue in Setif, where our clowning along with the music got the sort of applause that would normally only be heard at a Promenade Concert. After a week of performances in Setif, the whole concert party went on tour. It all came to an end in September when we embarked on HMS *Boxer*, headed back to war.

On 24 September we landed at Salerno and we were in action the same day. I remember being 'Stuka-ed'.

The evidence of this was a six-foot-deep trench at the bottom of which, looking up white-faced and saying 'Tell Hitler I'm sorry', was (by now) Lance Bombardier Milligan.

1944

By January we had seen some heavy fighting and we were positioned near

the village of Lauro. Along with four others, I had to take fresh batteries

Left:
SS Otranto.

Below:
A 7.2 of the 56th Heavy Regiment in action in Tunisia.

Above:

A Medium regiment comes ashore at Salerno on Red Beach where we landed.

Right:

D battery 7.2 in action under Monte Stellar.

(weighing 50lb) and a radio set to our O.P. at the top of Mount Dimiano. We had to negotiate a slope terraced for the olive trees. CRUMP! CRUMP! CRUMP! Mortars. We hit the ground.

CRUMP!

CRUMP!

CRUMP!

They stop.

Why? Can they see us? We get up and go on. CRUMP! CRUMP! CRUMP! He can see us! We hit the deck. A rain of them falling around us. I cling to the ground. I'll have a fag, that's what. I am holding a packet of Woodbines, then there is a noise like thunder. It's right on my head. There's a high pitched whistle in my ears. At first I black out and then I see red. I am strangely dazed. I was on my front, now I'm on my back, the red was opening my eyes straight into the sun. I know if we stay here we'll all die. I start to scramble down the hill.

Next I was at the bottom of the mountain, next I'm speaking to Major Jenkins, I am crying, I

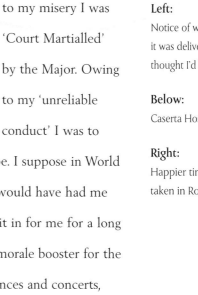

don't know why. He's saying, 'Get that wound dressed.' I said, 'What wound?' I had been hit on the side of my right leg. In a forward dressing station I am given sweet tea, two small white pills and a sticking plaster is put on the wound. I start to sway and am put on a stretcher. On a Red Cross truck we pass our artillery lines. I jump at each explosion.

I was labelled 'Battle Fatigue' at 144 CCS and sent to see a psychiatrist. He told me that I was going to get better but a week later I was back with the Battery. How I got back I don't know. This was a time of my life that I was very demoralised. I was not really me any more. I jumped every time our guns fired. I started stammering. To add to my misery I was 'Court Martialled' by the Major. Owing to my 'unreliable conduct' I was to relinquish my stripe. I suppose in World War I the bastard would have had me shot. He had had it in for me for a long time. I had been a morale booster for the boys, organising dances and concerts, always trying to keep a happy atmosphere, something he couldn't do. All this despite the fact the discharge certificate from

Left:

Notice of wounding. When it was delivered, my parents thought I'd been killed.

Below:

Caserta Hospital.

Right:

Happier times. A portrait taken in Rome.

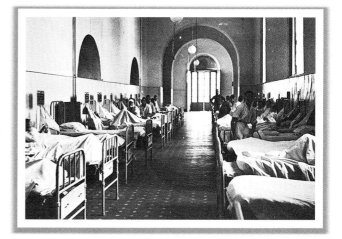

the 144 CCS had stated that 'This man must be rested behind the lines for a period to stabilise his condition.' I took the tranquillisers that they had given me. All they did was turn me into a zombie. I was now completely demoralised. I ended up in No 2 General Hospital, Caserta where I was seen by another psychiatrist. He sent me to a rehabilitation camp north of Naples.

After a couple of postings where I worked as a clerk and even a wine waiter in an officers' club, I found myself in Maddaloni where I met Sergeant Phil Phillips who led the O2E band. He asked me to play with them. Yes, yes, yes, yes! Now life took on a whole new meaning.

In early October we travelled by charabanc to Rome. We played at a dance in a huge marble hotel, an officers' dream palace. It was a cut above our regular Saturday night dance venues. I did my Christmas shopping that year in Naples.

Above:
Desmond, now serving in the Royal Ulster Rifles, Florence and Leo.

1945

On 1 May we were told the war was over! The energies of O2E were vested in preparations for the official V-E night celebrations. Part Two Orders: YOU WILL ALL HAVE A GOOD TIME. YOU WILL ALL GET DRUNK AND YOU WILL ALL STAGGER AROUND . . . YOU WILL GET SICK OVER EACH OTHER FOR YOUR KING AND COUNTRY. THE BAND WILL PLAY FOR DANCING UNTIL 2 A.M.

In July I was promoted to Bombardier and by October, when I

Below:

Practising in a corridor at the CPA barracks.

went home on leave to the UK, I had been made up to Sergeant. The four weeks spent with my parents and friends were over all too soon and on my return to Italy I was posted to the Central Pool of Artists, Welfare Department, Naples.

I was playing a borrowed guitar in a rehearsal room at the CPA barracks when I was approached by a tall

cadaverous gunner. This was Bill Hall. He played violin and he played it superbly. He was a virtuoso. But bloody scruffy. We teamed up just for the fun of it and in turn we were joined by Johnny Mulgrew, a short Scots lad from the Recce Corps. Together we sounded like *Le Club Hot de France*. When we played, other musicians would come and listen to us – a compliment – and it wasn't long before we were lined up for a show. In the filling-in time, I played trumpet in a scratch combination. We were playing for dancing at the Officers' Club in Naples when I met someone from Mars, Gunner Secombe, H., singer and lunatic, who had been pronounced loony after a direct hit from an 88mm gun in North Africa. He was part of the cabaret. He rushed on chattering, screaming, farting, sweat pouring off him like a monsoon. He wasn't an act, he was an interruption.

Top Left:
The lunatic Secombe in rehearsal.

Left:
O2E band with me seated second row, far right.

Above:

The Bill Hall Trio in our usual stage dress of carefully selected rags.

Right:

We were one incredible hit.

The Bill Hall Trio got its big break in a show called *Over The Page* which was staged at the Bellini Theatre on 6 December. We played and clowned and we were one incredible hit. When we came off, we were stunned. We continued to wow audiences in Bologna (where we spent Christmas), Florence, Bari and Naples.

1946

The Central Pool of Artists became The Combined Services Entertainment. Why? I suppose it was the result of a 'meeting'. The Bill Hall Trio was offered officer

---

Bill Hall Trio
MON. 17 JUNE 1946.
returns to Naples

WHETHER you are a lover of classical music or of swing, the news that the Bill Hall Trio is making a return visit to the Bellini Theatre in Naples is more than welcome, particularly after a week of curtailed entertainment.

They are appearing in the Central Pool of Artistes' show, *Barbary Coast*, the setting of which is a beer hall somewhere on the South Californian coast in the middle of the last century.

There are 38 players in the cast, which includes a troupe of dancers from the Royal Opera House in Rome, the popular comedian, Jimmy Malloy, and, playing the female lead as Frisco Lil, is Tiola Silenzi.

Old-stagers in Naples will remember the Bill Hall Trio in the CPA show, *Over the Page* when they played as gypsies, and their performance in the CMF Arts Festival.

I mentioned earlier that Naples is suffering from a week of curtailed entertainment. In future the Garrison Cinema will give only two shows daily, the afternoon matinees being discontinued. The revised hours are 1800 and 2030 hours.

In addition, the Bijou Cinema in Via Roma closes down after Wednesday night's performance of *Saratoga Trunk*.

status and wages if, when we were demobbed, we signed with the CSE for six months. I wrote to tell my parents and Mother proudly told the neighbours that her son was a 'Banjo-playing officer.'

In June a show called *Barbary Coast* opened at the Bellini Theatre. The Bill Hall Trio featured, as did the Italian Corps de Ballet, as did ballet dancer Maria Antoinetta Fontana – Toni. The first clash of eyes was enough. It

Above:
With Toni and in love.

Below:

Abroad the SS Dominion Monarch sailing far away from Toni.

was, no, not love at first sight – that came later – but it was most certainly *something* at first sight.

Our first date was on 27 June in the gardens of the Villa Borghese when the CSE were in Rome. From then on we were practically inseparable. Our budding romance was the talk of the company. We went sightseeing, swimming, shopping as the CSE toured through Padua, Venice, Trieste, on into Austria - Vienna and Graz, where one unforgettable night Toni and I consummated our love. When it was over, we lay quite still in the dark, then she started to cry.

'What's the matter, Toni?'

'I am different now. I am not girl any more.'

'Are you sorry?'

'No.'

With one act, everything was changed. We had made an invisible bond. Only time would tell its strength. I lay watching her dress in the half-light – every move was etched on my mind. I can still see it all quite clearly.

Bill Hall and I were officially demobbed in Austria and come September we were booked on the SS *Dominion Monarch* from Naples to the UK. Toni and I said our goodbyes in Rome and then countless times again by phone during the remaining days I had to spend in Naples. In Rome I had promised, 'I'll come back as soon as I can and write as much as I can.' It was not to be.

FAME, MARRIAGE AND FAMILY

1946

When I finally arrived home at my parents' house it was bitterly cold and there was heavy fog. I had wanted to surprise them and so didn't tell them I was coming. There was no-one home. This, plus the cold and gloom of winter in England made me very depressed.

1947

The Bill Hall trio played at various venues and created quite a stir. We got an agent and we were getting £75 a week. We thought we were millionaires! But I felt I needed to try something else and told Bill that I was quitting the act. The split was less than amicable. What he in fact said was, 'I hope you never get another fucking job again!' It was very venomous.

I went solo and had a wild act on stage. Normally a comic comes on to a

Fun with Laura, Sean. Baggage and a Davey Crockett hat.

real fanfare of upbeat music. For me, there was nothing. Then, from the back of the stage, wearing a pair of zip-up

This New Act Has A Big Future

Introducing . . .
The Bill Hall Trio

Here is the "Sporting Review's" first 1947 tip for future variety stardom—the Bill Hall Trio! An entire Spike Jones aggregation in miniature, these zany musicians really can play their instruments. Comedy and hot, pulsating rhythm goes hand in hand. The trio is led by—and christened by—Bill Hall, on violin. A pre-war single act, combining hot violinistics with dry humour, he met abroad Johnny Mulgrew, bass player of such bands as Stephan Grappelly's and the Ambrose Octette, and Spike Milligan, guitarist extraordinary. They grouped themselves together and became the sensational variety act of the Central Mediterranean Force abroad.
By a coincidence, they were featured in the same shows as another "Sporting Review" discovery now on the road to fame, Harry Secombe, who is one of their greatest "fans."
Currently playing the best night spots in Town, the Bill Hall Trio is a "natural" for our "new act" starved variety world.
In the exclusive pictures above, bass player Johnny Mulgrew is on the left, Spike Milligan strumming his guitar with Bill Hall listening in (centre), and on the right is "Maestro" Bill Hall himself, enthralling himself with his violin virtuosity (fiddling, to you!) JAN 1947

slippers, I'd appear going 'Der-dum, der-doh . . . der-doh, der-dum, . . .' in an Eccles-type voice.

Then I'd disappear again behind the back of the stage, 'Der-doh, der-doh, der-dum . . . der-dum, der-doh, dum, der-dum . . .' It took a lot of nerve, this.

Eventually, I'd make it to the microphone and say, 'I must be a big disappointment to you.'

And I used to wonder why I never got any work!

Above left:

Press cutting featuring The Bill Hall Trio, 1947.

Above:

Publicity postcard drawn by Bill Hall.

Right:

Romeo.

1948

I auditioned for Ann Lenner, who was forming a trio. I passed the audition playing the guitar and singing. The third member of the act was Red O'List, whom I had met during the war in Italy when he was a Captain in the CSE. We joined a show called *Swinging Along* with Eddie Molloy, a comedian who was about as funny as a brick, and set off to tour Germany and Austria.

We sailed to the Hook of Holland and from there on to Hamburg, or what was left of it. The chorus girls travelled with us. I took up with a stunning redhead, Dorita Trent. Eventually we were sleeping together. Our first show was at the Opera House in Hamburg.

It was an exhausting tour, two shows and all night with Dorita. The tour finished in Vienna and from there we headed home. I then went solo

again, but carried on screwing Dorita.

I did a Hughie Green talent spotting radio show – nothing happened.

Left:
Dorita, the chorus girl on the left who stopped me wanking.

Below:
Ann Lenner Trio – there were three of us.

Above:
I played the comic part – Hello,
Sailor!

The landlord of the Grafton Arms
in Sutton Ground, Westminster, was
struggling to write scripts for what was
the world's un-funniest man (possibly
even less funny than Eddie Molloy),
Derek Roy, who sang for Geraldo's
band. Somehow, he was appearing on
what was Britain's most popular radio
show, *Variety Band Box*. Roy got his
laughs by putting funny wigs on with
the punch line. Great for radio.

I had met up again with Harry
Secombe, who was by now appearing at
the Windmill, and he introduced me to
Michael Bentine, who had introduced
Harry to the Grafton Arms. I'd meet

```
Telegrams:                ALLIED HIGH COMMISSION PERMIT OFFICE
Hypoff, Southkens,                    FOR GERMANY,
London.                   HAUTE COMMISSION ALLIEE en ALLEMAGNE
                           BUREAU de PERMIS de VOYAGE,
Telephone:                    22-25, PRINCES GARDENS,
KENsington 4511 Ext.             SOUTH KENSINGTON,
                                 LONDON, S.W.7.
Our Reference:
                          (Nearest Stn:  South Kensington)
Your Reference:           (Nearest Buses: Nos. 9.73 & 74)
                          Office Hours: Monday-Friday 9.30 - 4.00
                                        Saturday 9.30 - 11.30.

                          Date   17. 3. 1950.

SUBJECT: EUCOM Facilities for   Mr Terence Alan
                                   MILLIGAN.

        The above-mentioned person is authorized Occupational

Facilities in the US Area of Control in Germany under the pro-

visions of EUCOM Circular No. 2, paragraph 6,A dated 13 May, 1949,

per authority contained   EUCOM SIGNAL No: SC 14306

                          dated 15. 3. 1950.


                                        E.B. Sutton
(SEAL)                                  US Permit Officer
```

killed every one. Derek Roy killed 99% of all known jokes, but Grafton thought my stuff was funny.

Then I got a break. The BBC wanted a Derek Roy half hour and, surprisingly, he wanted me in it. The show was called *Hip Hip Hoo Roy*. I had to do an idiot voice which later developed into Eccles for *The Goons*.

Left:
Me wowing them at the Metropole Theatre, Edgware Road.

Above:
Authorisation to visit occupied Germany to entertain G.I.s, 1950.

Right:
Must change my washing powder.

Harry there, I would play piano and Harry would sing. One night in the bar I was telling Harry and Michael some of my own jokes. Grafton overheard me, we got talking and he asked me if I would like to write with him. All my jokes were far out and Derek Roy

1949

I moved into the attic above Grafton's. There were three attic sections. I was in one with my typewriter, still turning out jokes which Derek Roy didn't use. I was paid £3 or £4 for him not to use my jokes and continued writing for this remuneration. I used to hear a noise in the attic next door. I looked through the keyhole and there was a monkey looking back at me. Jimmy Grafton had bought it as a present for his wife. We made friends, but later the monkey bit me, so they locked it in the garage.

I went to see Harry appearing at the Hackney Empire and in the bar he introduced me to Peter Sellers. Peter wanted to look like a male model – posh suit, posh collar and tie, Macintosh, gloves he carried in his left hand . . . oh, and a trilby hat. He was very softly spoken – I thought I was going deaf! I was very impressed by his countenance. He was quite

Above:
Bentine, me and Sellers clowning for the camera. Secombe always looked like that.

Below:

We are introduced to the
BBC Radio Personality of the
Year, 1951.

dignified, apart from the fact that he didn't buy a bloody drink all night. Dignified but skint! Eventually he did put his hand in his pocket . . . and pulled out a handkerchief. Harry, on the other hand, spent his entire night's takings on alcohol for me and Peter. Peter then joined us as a regular at the Grafton,

doing impressions.

Peter became a particularly close friend because he had such a mad, abstract mind. He was a very, very likeable man when you got to know him. He had a tape recorder and we started recording funny voices. We discovered that, by slowing down the

recording, you could play it back very quickly. We all thought the speeded up voices were hilarious.

I was still working as musician, playing with bands in a variety of shows, but more and more time was being spent experimenting with Peter, Harry and Michael – with the encouragement of Jimmy Grafton. This was the start of *The Goons*.

1951

Peter and Harry had been getting work on radio with the BBC and Peter had a contact with a producer called Pat Dixon. He was an innovator. He did *Breakfast With Braden*, *Bedtime With Braden* and *Brass Hatters Band*. He didn't really show much interest in us at first but I think he felt there was

Left:
On the stairs, refusing to be thrown out of Broadcasting House.

Above:
Michael left *The Goons* in 1952. The great rift that everyone believed had grown between us was much exaggerated.

Junior Crazy Gang! The first show was broadcast on 28 May as *The Crazy People*. It wasn't until the second season that we eventually forced them to call it *The Goon Show*.

a spark of talent that needed to be recognised, so I went away and wrote the crappiest script ever. Crappy, but totally new and unusual.

With Pat Dixon's support, we were given the chance to record a pilot show. Actually, this was the second time we had recorded a pilot, but the first one had been turned down by the planners. This time, Pat pressured them into giving us the go-ahead.

Do you know what those sons of fun at the BBC wanted to call us? *The*

Peter had been in a recording studio before and so had Harry and Michael. I was the only one outside the pale. I didn't really think anything about it; I was so worried in case no one liked the script. The audience didn't understand a word of it. God bless the band; they saved it. They were all muzos and they really dug the jokes.

Not many people know that my girlfriend, Margaret McMillan, was in the first show. I didn't know that the first show would be the first of two

hundred shows. I didn't know that I had that much in me.

Round this time Peter had the hots for a girl called Anne Howe. He was going to meet her and a friend at the Edgewarebury Club. First we had to pick up her friend, June. We knocked on the door and something that knocked me off my feet appeared in the doorway, wrapped in the briefest of towels. She was Italian, huge dark eyes, black hair, huge boobs. Yes, she was for me! We were soon going steady.

In November, having decided to emigrate, my parents sailed for Australia.

1952

On 26 January June Marlow and I were married. We were very happy together, but eventually the strain I was under in writing *The Goon Show* would tear us apart.

There were constant battles with the BBC. We did a whole spectrum of voices on the show. Peter could do anything from a dustman to the Queen,

Above:
The wedding party, January 1952.

Below:

Joy! A daughter! Laura is born on 2 November 1952.

but the BBC didn't like us doing voices like General Montgomery, Churchill or the Queen. They only wanted jokes like, 'I used to play the Palladium.' 'Yes, I've never heard it played better.'

I was writing at our flat in Shepard Hill Road but when my daughter, Laura, came along, she distracted me so much I found an office at 137 Shepherds Bush Road. I would take

the Underground from Archway and change at Camden for Shepherds Bush. It was a short walk to the office which I shared with Eric Sykes. I had bought a Letra 22 typewriter (I still have it) and I worked a long day, leaving home at 9 a.m. in the morning and working until ten or eleven at night, sometimes I worked through the night. I had to work long hours to make the scripts as good as I could. When I got home, June would have left out a meal for me to warm up. I had difficulty sleeping and I was seen by a stupid doctor who kept giving me sleeping pills – you name 'em, I've taken 'em.

This life put a great strain on me and my marrige with a wonderful wife, June. I must have behaved impossibly – it was all leading up to a breakdown.

In December I was writing the third series of *Goon Shows* when I finally broke down. If anybody wants to know what down is, ask me – I've been there. The doctor who was treating me realised that I was too much for him to handle and had me taken to St Luke's

Psychiatric Hospital in Muswell Hill in London. As I got out of the ambulance, there was a cat sitting on the doorstep. I stroked it. The contact with its fur was

soothing. They put me in a room next to a noisy bloody kitchen. I screamed 'Get me out of here!' A doctor gave me a jab of something and in ten seconds I was unconscious. I lay there in a deep sleep for fourteen days.

They brought me round occasionally to drink some liquid food. I grew a dark brown beard and I remember one nurse saying, 'He looks like our Lord.' When I was half awake I had hallucinations. Hanging from the ceiling were halves of coat hangers. Then there was a live lion on top of the cupboard. There came a stream of silver, materialising in the doorway opposite into a lady with black ribbon round her hair, which hung down to her shoulders.

Left:
Me lurking in the background, feeling the pressure (will it get a laugh?) as Peter and Harry perform one of my scripts.

Above:
Me before the breakdown.

Right:
Me after the breakdown.

The trauma of my childhood bed wetting haunted me and even though I couldn't pass any urine, I'd keep on trying, still unconscious. The result, a prolapse.

One good thing came from all this. I was a heavy smoker and being unconscious for two weeks had abated the craving. A nurse would sit with me all night. She smoked, I smelled it. Deep down I wanted to give up and now was the chance. I took it – I've never really smoked since.

June came to visit. She looked terrible with worrying about the bread winner having come to a sudden halt.

1953

By February I was well enough to leave hospital, but still very shaky. I went back to the slog of writing which I faithfully did, although the payment was very small. For my acting part in the show I think I got £12 and for writing I got £25. As Sellers and Secombe were big names they got £100 a week. Ultimately, I was paid £100 as well and,

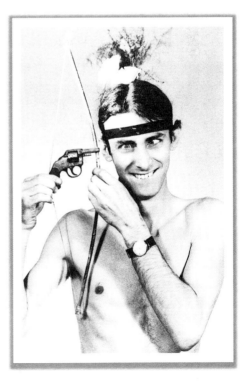

with repeats, £200 – a lot of money. £200 – that must have hurt them!

By now Michael Bentine had left *The Goons*. He was an extraordinary character who told the most extraordinary stories. He once told me that his mother had levitated from the ground, across the dining room table and settled on the other side. One night when we were appearing in a show in Birmingham, I asked him, as he claimed to be a mathematician, could he give me the formula for the atomic bomb?

He took out a lipstick and covered the mirror in the dressing room with Pythagoras, finishing off at the bottom on the right hand side with, 'There! That is the formula for the atomic bomb!' Unfortunately, there was a Professor Penny in the audience that night. I happened to know him and he came into the dressing room and looked at the mirror. I asked him what it was and he said, 'That's a load of bollocks!' I told Michael and he said, 'Of course it is! You don't think I would give away the secret of the atom bomb to you in a dressing room in Birmingham, do you?'

1954

On 17 September we had a second child, Sean Patrick. Joy, a boy! At least one successor to my name!

Left:
Sean, my successor – he's the one on the right.

Right:
Baggage, Sean, June, Laura and me in Holden Road.

Far Right:
Going on holiday in 'Little Min'.

We bought a Maltese puppy and called him Baggage. He was scruffy but cute. Also scruffy but cute was the 1929 Austin soft top tourer which I bought from Peter Sellers for £300.

1955

We bought, on a mortgage, 127 Holden Road, Finchley. It had a large garden with a stream at the bottom. That summer June took Laura and Sean on holiday in the car, by now named

'Little Min'. I couldn't go as I was still working hard to deliver a complete *Goon Show* script once a week.

1956

This year saw me start to venture into writing for television. First there was *The Idiot Weekly Priced 2d*, then *A Show Called Fred* was transmitted in May and in September came the sequel, *Son Of Fred*. I was awarded Best TV Show Of The Year for the *Fred* shows, although there were only about 350 TV sets in England at the time, so nobody really noticed. I had to borrow Eric Sykes' dinner suit for the award ceremony. I was given rapturous applause, but I think most of it was for *The Goon Shows*.

Fred also featured Harry Edgington on piano with the band of the Massed Alberts in numbers where we danced in dustbins singing:

When you're feeling lonely

And you can't find romance

Jump into a dustbin . . . and dance

When you've got no trousers

And ragged underpants

Jump into a dustbin . . . and dance

This year there were also records – 'The Ying Tong Song' was released as well as 'I'm Walking Backwards For Christmas' and 'Bloodnock's Rock And Roll Call'. There was a film, too – *The Case Of The Muckinese Battlehorn*. A busy year with unending pressure.

Above:
A large garden and a pussy cat, Laura at Holden Road.

Right:
The happy, smiley *Goons*.

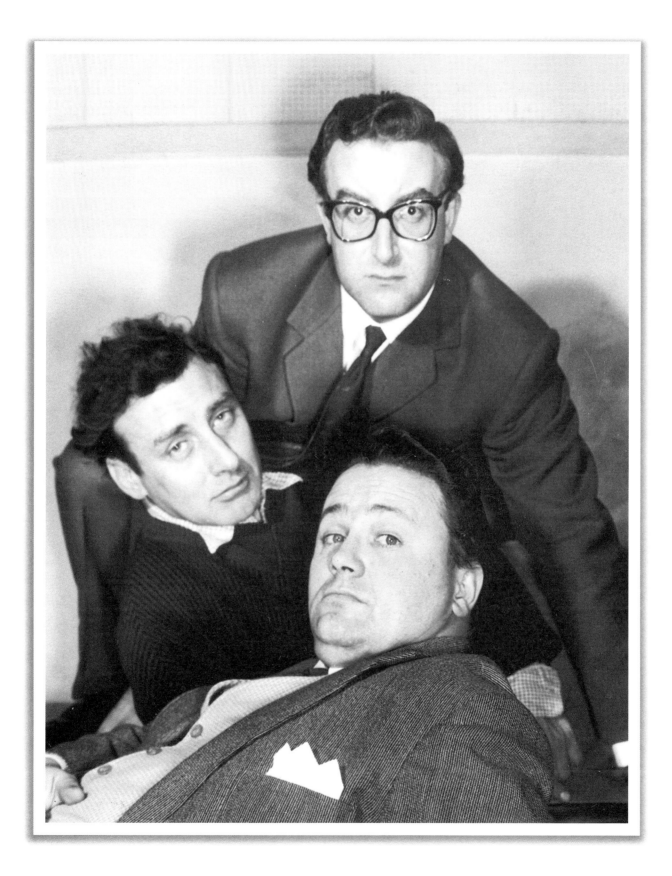

gravel. I tried to transform that and I had to fight like mad and people didn't like me for it. I had to rage and bang and crash. In the end it paid off but it drove me mad in the process – it drove a lot of other people mad as well! I don't think I could be a success again at that same level because I just couldn't go through all the tantrums.

1957

The Goon Show was going from strength to strength. Audiences loved it. We used to attract a certain type of audience who understood our style of humour. Sometimes the laughter was like being given a course of vitamins, it felt that good.

I started to shake the BBC out of its apathy. Sound effects used to be a knock on the door and a trudge on

1958

I was commissioned to write a comedy series for the Australian Broadcasting Commission.

Below:
First surviving picture of Silé, who was born on 2 December 1957.

Above:
Kidnapped!

June, the children and I sailed from London on the P&O liner *Arcadia*. At Melbourne, I was mobbed by students. They said I was to be kidnapped, taken ashore and ransomed for the princely sum of $1 to be paid by the ship's captain. Some bloody press photographer also wanted me to look out the porthole and 'Stick yer arse out!' So I did. I shouted to him, 'Good luck in your next job.'

I stayed for a while with my Mum and Dad at 393 Orange Grove Road, Woy Woy. It was a very small waterside

town but wonderful and completely surrounded by bush.

My family moved into a cliff-top home over-looking Bilgola Bay. One day the owner came round demanding an advance of rent. I said I hadn't been paid yet by the ABC. She said, 'Then get out!' So we got out and moved to a home in Avalon. There, in a terrible mood, I threatened to strike June. The children were all disturbed by the shouting.

We had hired a car which June drove. She came home late one evening. I discovered her knickers in the glove compartment. I didn't know what to think.

I took my parents to a posh restaurant at Kingscross called The Georgian. When my mother saw the prices on the menu, she nearly fainted. I nearly fainted when we discovered that the Australian nanny who was looking after Silé had a criminal record!

Desmond (who had emigrated to Australia with Mum and Dad) and his wife, Nadia, used to spend weekends with our parents. Desmond saw

Left:
Laura's 6th birthday party. Laura, Sean and Silé all marked with a cross I would have to bear.

Below:
Leo persuading Desmond to commit suicide.

Above:
Daddy pays a visit for
Silé's birthday.

the new 'log cabin' I had had built for Dad's gun collection. When I was in the money I had arranged for it to be built on the back verandah at Orange Grove Road. One wall was all wooden lengths to be used to display Leo's collection of old muskets and pistols.

1959

We continued to live at 127 Holden Road, but I was behaving abominably towards June. It must have come as some relief when I was booked for a return visit to Australia to write another show for ABC. I sailed on my own on a Dutch ship.

While I was in Woy Woy I wrote my first book, *Silly Verse For Kids*. On my return to England I would show it to publisher Dennis Dobson. He published it and it was a great success. It went on and on being reprinted.

Also while in Woy Woy, I got a telegram saying that June had left our home and taken the children with her. My reaction was to stage a token suicide attempt. I had some sleeping tablets and I took quite a large number. I think this was really a cry for help.

June had found a lover and moved to Maze Road in Richmond. When I got home, I was allowed to visit on Silé's birthday, 2 December 1959. I took her a teddy bear and a birthday cake. She was totally aware of the break-up of our marriage.

This year I also wrote a book of serious poetry called *Values*. God knows what it was about. I think it was about 30 pages.

By Christmas the children were stilll at Maze road. I set up a Christmas tree in my office and they came to see me there. I gift wrapped all their presents and put big white card labels on them.

Over Christmas, the children and I spent time with Eric Sykes and his family in Surrey. One night I gave all of Eric's family and all of my lot each a torch. I was Will O' The Wisp. I had a torch with a red bulb which I flashed occasionally as I ran through the woods. It was great fun with lots of laughing and squealing. The children were very happy and I took as much of that as I could get.

It had been the most traumatic year of my life. I had become famous and successful, but deeply unhappy. God please help me.

Left:
You can tell by Sean and Laura's sad faces how the marriage break-up was affecting them.

Right:
Me doing my best, which isn't good enough.

Below:
This photo says it all.

NEW HOPES
AND NEW
BEGINNINGS

1960

I hired a private detective and had June's home in Richmond watched. Her lover stayed with her at night and would leave very early in the morning. I had the detective with me as a witness when I caught him leaving. Adultery in those days was a social crime. I petitioned for divorce naming him as co-respondent.

On 28 January, the final *Goon Show* was transmitted, although it would continue to be repeated throughout the 1960s. Various *Goon Shows* have been released on LPs, on cassette, even on CD, but for years the BBC have left the shows lying on a shelf gathering dust, rather than broadcast them again for the young people who have never heard the shows on radio. I live in hope.

In June, came Laura's first Communion. Dutifully, I was there.

Smears! Useless bloody
window cleaner!

1961

On 10 March the divorce was finalised and I was given custody of the children.

Of course, June was seen as the guilty party, having committed adultery. They didn't say anything about me being fucking mad, insane, unstable, suicidal. That was okay. You could have three kids and look after them when you were like that.

I took Laura, Sean and Silé back to live with me in Holden Road, fully realising that I had parted them from a very good mother. To this day that haunts me, but her lover was a rough, crude man and the children would have grown up the same. I did my very best for them. I sent them to private schools and convents. I had a housekeeper, Mrs Ferguson, and an Irish nanny, Miss O'Brien.

June never visited the children.

Above left:
The bride of Christ.

Above:
Swinging Communion girl.

Above:

Miss O'Brien (left) and
Mrs Ferguson (right) with
my three treasures.

Above right:

Sean's first Communion.

Her excuse was that I never gave her money for petrol. All news to me.

Sean's first Communion came in June and I was there, just as I had been for Laura. It was about this time, too, that I played a part in a World War II film, *Invasion Quartet*, with Bill Travers. It was desperately unfunny. I had appeared in other films over the last ten years, *Let's Go Crazy* with Peter Sellers and the 'Goon' movies. *Penny Points To Paradise, Down Among The Z Men* and *Muckinese Battlehorn*, so what was so special about this one? Well, the one thing that came of it was that I saw a very pretty, shapely girl extra. I asked her out to dinner. Her name was Patricia (Paddy) Ridgeway.

Left:
Paddy, my love.

Above:
Paddy in *The Sound of Music.*

Right:
Me, heavily disguised to
avoid creditors.

We got on very well.
By now, of course, I was
a free man with three
children, a cook and a
nanny. The short of it was,
we fell in love. At the time
she was appearing as a nun
in *The Sound Of Music.* I
went to see it. My God,
she had a wonderful voice.

I introduced her to all my children
and she took me up to Menston to
meet her mother and father. He was
a director in Monsanto, the huge
chemical company. They seemed to
accept me as a nice 'boy'.

In December, I was surprised to
get a letter from Sir Bernard Miles
asking me if I would play the part of
Ben Gunn in *Treasure Island.* I was
delighted and played the part as a
half-mad old man. I was well received
by the audience.

1962

My great romance with Paddy was
leading up to a wedding which took
place on 26 April in St Joseph's Roman
Catholic Church, Cragwood. The best

man was George Martin. I think he still is. I still am. Harry Secombe was in the congregation. As Paddy and I stood at the altar, I put on a big, black handlebar moustache and turned to the congregation. It did get a laugh, but Paddy's father took me aside at the reception and said, 'What a terrible thing to do at my daughter's wedding!' <u>Her</u> wedding? I was there, too!

For our honeymoon we went to Cornwall, where we stayed at The Lobster Pot, recommended to us by Roger Hancock (Tony's brother and agent) – it was terrible!

Paddy came to live with us in Holden Road and, for a time, we were very happy. Silé, who was too young to remember much about June, grew up with Paddy as her mother. One thing I disagreed with Paddy about was the schooling of the children. She wanted them to go to a boarding school, very Victorian. I partly agreed. Laura went to a convent and came home at weekends. Sean went to a local private school, St Mary's Abbey Convent. I remember the name – I also remember the bills! Silé went to kindergarten.

Left:
Such a nice couple.

Below:
Hooked.

Above:
Who's first?

Right:
Paddy and I leaving for
the honeymoon

Above:
The wedding party, including
best man George Martin.

Left:

The Goon show was finished, but the laughs continued, as in this TV appearance with Peter.

Left:

June Thorburn after my sausage at a party in the *Mermaid Theatre*, 1962.

Top right:

Recording the voices for the BBC's *Telegoons* puppet show version of *The Goon Show* in 1963.

Right:

And examining the puppets.

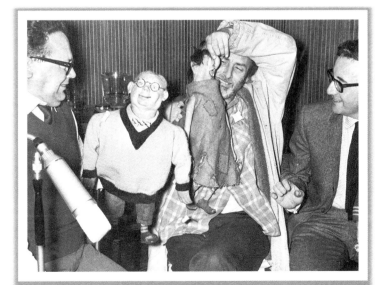

The Goon Show was now finished, although it would continue to crop up in various forms. We even gave a special performance on one of Harry's TV shows. *The Goons* had been at the top so I had said, sadly, FINIS. It had run from April 1951. It had made me famous, made me ill, destroyed my first marriage and, although Paddy was now fulfilling the role, it had left my three children without a mother. It is still hell to think about it.

On 11 May 1962, I booked the P & O liner *Canberra*, travelling with Paddy in a stateroom to Australia. I was booked by the ABC to do another *Idiots Weekly* series for them. Alas, the children had to stay behind in the care of their nanny. The trip did, however, afford us the opportunity to visit my parents.

Above left:
Me in *A Series Of Unrelated Incidents At Current Market Value*, 1961.

Above:
An officer at last, but only in the dreadfully unfunny film *Invasion Quartet*.

Right:
Aboard the *Canberra* bound for Australia with the children's paintings decorating our stateroom.

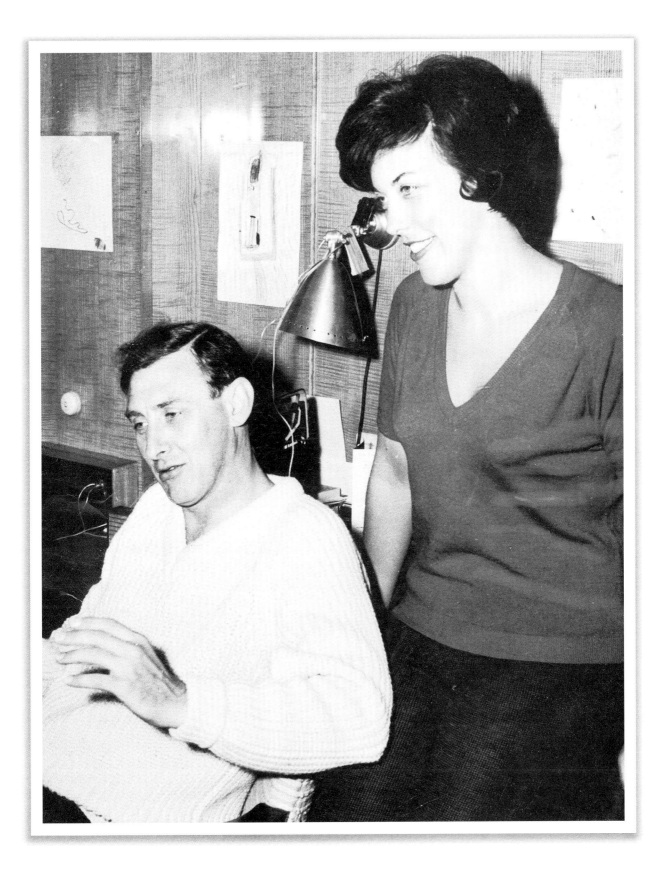

1963

Never tiring of a life on the ocean waves, in the summer of 1963, the whole family set sail on the SS *Lakonia* for a holiday cruise.

Left:
My father looking for a handout.

Below:
Silé, Sean and Laura line up to welcome us home.

They were still living in Woy Woy and they were very happy there. We weren't.

Paddy nearly drove me mad with constant bickering. One night I ran out of the house and slept in a bus shelter.

By December, we were back home to rejoin the children and resume family life. Laura, Sean and Silé were there to greet us, parading in front of the blackboard wall I had painted for them to draw on. There were always many wonderful and weird drawings on that blackboard.

Above:
Walking as slowly as possible to avoid the Captain's cocktail party.

Above right:
The Tub – it later sank!

Right:
Laura and me preparing for the ship to sink.

Oh, the agony of the captain's cocktail party. He didn't speak very good English and he didn't serve very good wine. He kept absenting himself from the party – I think he went to see if the engines were still working. They weren't! We had to stop at Madeira for the engines to be mended. To the delight of the children, and to my terror, we went on a terrifying downhill run on one of the sleds for which Madeira is famous.

During one of the cabaret nights on the cruise,

Paddy and Barry Kent (of Churchill's Club) sang 'I'll Walk Alone'. Tremendous reception!!!

There was also a children's fancy-

dress contest. Silé won it dressed as a lady of fashion, wearing false eye lashes, lipstick and rouge, furs and one of Paddy's wide-brimmed hats.

Back in London, Paddy came home one day with a puppy for the family. The kids were overjoyed. They called it Pom-Pom and exhausted the poor thing within minutes of it crossing the threshold.

This year I wrote another book, *The Little Pot Boiler* and also had my first novel published – *Puckoon*. I had started *Puckoon* in 1958 and doodled with it for four years. It nearly

drove me mad and I vowed I'd never write another novel. The book was set in Ireland because I had the notion that I wanted to be known as an Irish writer, Unfortunately, nobody really knew I was Irish!

Paddy appeared in a Midnight Matinee show, *The Merry Widow*, at Sadlers Wells, and also took a trip to Paris to see *The Folies Bergère* with two friends, Dougie Squires and Jamie Phillips. I had too much on to go with them. A play written

Top left:
The terrifying downhill sledge run.

Above:
Silé receives the children's fancy dress prize from an adult who lost in his contest.

Left:
Pom-Pom overwhelmed by overjoyous children.

Right:
Paddy as a show girl. Oh, those legs!

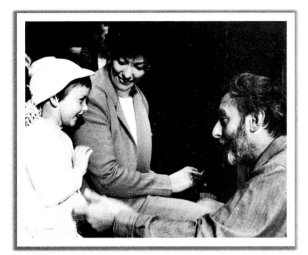

tea in bed and sang Happy Birthday.
I bought her a splendid necklace and
took her to Kettner's for dinner, then
on to Danny la Rue's nightclub. They
had a twee floor show with the then
unknown comic, Ronnie Corbett.

On 26 April, Paddy and I celebrated
our second wedding anniversary. I
took the whole family to the ballet at
Covent Garden. It was *Swan Lake* –
wonderful. Then we went on to dinner
at Kettner's (again – the expense!)
where the children drank our health
and Alfredo, an old-time waiter, sang us
a Neopolitan folk tune, 'Vacine Mare
Vacina More'.

by myself and John Antrobus was to
be staged at the Mermaid Theatre. I
remember that, during one rehearsal,
Paddy and Silé visited me – oh, such a
darling daughter. *The Bed Sitting Room*
opened at the Mermaid to good notices.
I had noticed. It transferred to the
West End, to the Comedy Theatre.

Top left:
Rehearsals for *The Bed Sitting Room* and a visit from my darling daughter, Silé.

Bottom left:
The kittens in the box the children made.

1964

It was Paddy's
birthday on
8 February, so
I brought her

A couple of
days later, the cat
had kittens. The
mother, Fluffy

Bum, cleaned them constantly. The children made a box to keep the kittens

anniversary. They had a dinner at Desmond's home in Sydney. I'm not sure whether they were celebrating the hotel room wedding or the church wedding – probably both.

They arrived at Tilbury in May. I had arranged for a car to bring them home. They arrived and the whole family made a huge fuss of them and settled them in the big double bedroom. It must all have seemed a ploy because, as soon as

Above:
The moment before the POP! Mum and Dad celebrate 50 years of marriage with Desmond (taking the photo) and Nadia.

Right:
The Captain's cocktail party, Leo wearing the evening dress I paid for!

in. It was pandemonium! All this with my parents due to arrive to stay with us, too!

I had booked a first class passage for my parents on the P & O *Himalaya* to the UK, returning on the *Canberra*. Prior to departing for London, Florence and Leo celebated their 50th wedding

I contacted Peter Scott at slimbridge Wild Fowl sanctuary and asked him for a cob. It was

they had got their feet under the table, Paddy and I were off on holiday. With the grandparents babysitting, Paddy and I took a cruise on the *Canberra*. We visited Naples, Greece and Istanbul.

In Athens, Paddy met an old boyfriend. He was fat and BALD. I was delighted. We came home refreshed, and went straight into organising a party for Sean's tenth birthday.

Good deed! On the Totteridge Pond there was a lone female swan.

delivered and released on the pond. It worked! Together, next spring, they hatched four cygnets!

Beatles producer, George Martin made a comedy LP record with me called *Milligan Preserved*. I don't think it sold very well, but it was very, very funny. It was also good to know I had been preserved.

We took my mum and dad to shows in London. They enjoyed the London Palladium best but one which

Top left:
Mum and Dad had never seen their grandchildren before. The picture includes me so they know who did it.

Top:
Hiding my skinny body behind a towel.

Above:
Paddy, shocked by her old boyfriend.

Right:
The pond before the arrival of the cob.

'It's done us all a power of good,' said my father, no longer troubled nowadays with any kind of inflammations in his soft palate.

In September, my parents returned to Australia first class on the *Canberra*.

Left:
Sean's 10th birthday. He got a bike, which you can just see here. I had to hide it in the garage for a week.

Below:
Recording *Milligan Preserved*. George Martin canonizing me.

left them particularly bemused was an avant-garde play by a hippy writer, one Noel Atkins. My parents didn't understand it. After it finished my dad said, 'What the bloody hell was that about?' I said, '£5 a seat.'

I dined them at Kettner's where, at one time, King Edward brought his lady friends. My mother liked that bit of news.

One evening, my mum cooked a real hot Indian curry; next day we all had the shits.

Above:
My children swimming to entertain my mother.

Right:
My father typing a letter of complaint to the Captain.

They were waited on hand and foot by two stewards – just like the old days. They arrived in Sydney and travelled by train, steam train in those days, to Woy Woy. The one hour journey took them through the most wonderful territory of the Kurangai Chase National Park and over the giant Hawkesbury River. Almost as soon as they were home, Dad sent me a picture of him in his gun room.

In December, I became a West End star in a show called *Son of Oblomov*. This had originally started as a straight play at the New Lyric Theatre, Hammersmith. Alas, at every rehearsal the cast changed the script. The result: the first night I couldn't remember the script so I ad-libbed into comedy. It was so successful that it transferred to the Comedy Theatre where it played to packed houses, breaking the box office records!

Another family Christmas. I had three large stockings made; red for Laura, yellow for Sean, green for Silé. We waited till they were all asleep, then hung them over their door knobs. The stockings were full of little novelties, cards, sweets, a little toy and an apple and an orange.

Laura's big present was a dressing table. Sean had an air rifle and shot at everything in the garden. Hell on legs! Silé had a lovely dolls' house. She was totally in love with it. All the presents were opened around the Christmas tree. We had a traditional lunch, turkey, etc., all of us bursting, then retired to

the front room where I played the guitar and Paddy sang. I also recited some comedy poems:

Left:
Promoting a single, *Sideways Through The Sewers Of The Strand* from the *Milligan Preserved* album.

Top:
Leo trying to price a flintlock for sale.

Top right:
Laura and present – it cost £53!

Right:
Doll's house and proud home owner.

My name is Fred Fernacker Pan

I walk about the town

Sometimes with my trousers up

And sometimes with 'em down.

And when they were up they were up

And when they were down they were

down

And when they were only halfway up

I was arrested.

Then Laura sang 'Sea Shells':

Sea shells

Sing me a song of the sea

A song of ships and sailings

Of islands and tropical seas

Of pirates on the Spanish Main

Which no man shall see again.

And then Sean:

Not last night

But the night before

Three tom-cats came

Top left:

Sile's Christmas card to Santa Claus.

Left:

My new series, *Muses With Milligan*, a mixture of poetry and jazz, began on BBC 2 on Christmas Day.

Above:
Out and about in our Mini,
1965. I've always liked Minis
and still have one.

Bottom left:
Cornwall ahoy!

Bottom right:
The white balcony behind
Paddy is our honeymoon spot.

Knocking at the door

One with a trumpet

One with a drum

And one with a pancake

Stuck to his bum.

Then mince pies and tea – ah,

Christmas memories.

1965

8 February, Paddy's birthday. I
bought her some gold earrings.
That evening I took her to dinner
at Kettner's, then to Danny la
Rue's (again). I opened a bottle of
champagne for her. Very romantic.

In the spring, Paddy took all the
children on holiday in Cornwall.
She wanted them to see the Lobster
Pot Inn where we had spent our
honeymoon. She took them sightseeing
everywhere. They saw the sunrise
over the sea, before visiting the fish
market to watch the trawlers bring in
their catches.

THE ELFIN OAK

This is a story all on its own. One day I took Laura to see the Elfin Oak in Kensington Gardens. It was in a ruinous state. It had originally been carved by Ivor Cutler, who had used the contours of the tree to carve little pixies, fairies, goblins, witches – some one hundred of them. The tree was then in Richmond deer park where it had been killed by lightning. Rutting deer would sharpen their horns on it. Cutler, a sculptor, saw the chance to use the gnarled trunk to carve the fairies and other creatures. When he had completed it, the then Home Secretary, George Lansbury, saw the finished work and had it replanted in Kensington where for thirty years it had slowly deteriorated.

As we stood there, Laura said, 'What a shame. Why doesn't someone mend it?' That was to be me. I wrote to the Ministry of Public Works and they authorised me to restore it. A friend, Doug Rouse, had two sets of wood carving tools. It was a start. He and my wartime friend, Harry Edgington,

Left:
Screens and roof in place.

Top:
Sustenance to keep the workers happy

Above:
Hard at work with a little helper.

168

This page:
Before and after shots of
a figure climbing the tree.

started work. First we had a screen and a roof erected around the tree.

We had to strip all the old paint off the figures. I bought 400 dolls' glass eyes. These we fixed into each figure. We filled in all the cracks with a self-hardening agent and, where parts were missing, I restored them. Then they were sandpapered. We wrote to the Managing Director of British Paints and asked for twenty different colours. They

gave them to us gratis.

Pretty good. Next we wanted
Rentokil to spray against woodworm.
They did it gratis. To secure the tree
we had to concrete in the roots.
The builders, Murphy, did it gratis.
Now each figure had to be painted.

For three years we worked. The
finished tree looked marvellous. It
was unveiled in 1965 by the Prince
of Wales.

This page:
One of the figures in three
stages of restoration.

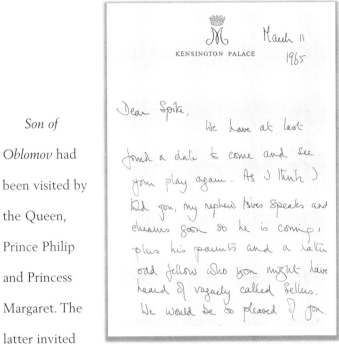

Right:
The letter inviting us to
dinner at Kensington Palace!

Below:
Children and kittens writing
letters to be hand delivered
to the Queen.

*Son of
Oblomov* had
been visited by
the Queen,
Prince Philip
and Princess
Margaret. The
latter invited
us to dinner with 'my sister' at
Kensington Palace. Wow! It was a
lovely dinner served by waiters whom
Margaret seemed to
ignore completely.

For our summer
holidays this year we
went to a villa
owned by Eric Sykes,
near Malaga, in
Spain. He lent it to
us. He is a nice man. On the shore by
the beach there was a sort of little bar
with a roof. The owner and his wife
served various iced drinks and, of
course, sangria. They were a really nice
couple. I had an idea; could he and his
wife make paella one evening for Paddy
and me. For that evening (Laura was
babysitting), Paddy wore an evening
gown and I black tie. They were so
pleased to see us dressed up. They had
arranged a table with a white tablecloth.

They brought crockery and set the table with napkins, cutlery and two chairs (essential, really). They served us themselves and opened a bottle of red wine. When we finished we drank a toast to them. Then Paddy, with that magnificent voice, sang Mozart and an aria from *Madam Butterfly*. They applauded, then he sang Spanish folk songs, with clouds of garlic. An unforgettable evening.

There were some magical moments like this, but there were some hellish rows, too. Paddy could have a terrible temper, as could I, and at one point there were continual rows, one after another. She even shouted at Laura, 'Get out of this house!' This was too much for Laura, who resented Paddy from then on and our relationships became very strained.

Then Paddy's father said to me in private, 'Spike, this woman wants a baby.' I promised I'd do my best.

Top left:
The family at Eric Sykes's villa in Spain.

Below left:
Another Roman Catholic! Silé in Confirmation White.

As well as the TV appearances, scriptwriting and all of the other things in which I

The nuns said it was time for 'dear little Silé's confirmation', so here we go again. Another innocent being forced to become a Roman Catholic.

was involved, this year I had two books published – *A Book Of Bits Or A Bit Of A Book* and *A Dustbin Of Milligan*. They both did quite well.

Above:

Leo shooting a neighbour.

Above right:

Leo, Desmond, Florence, Nadia and Mrs Klun at the end of their Christmas lunch, drinking a toast to the photographer.

Right:

He doesn't know it yet, but his name is Michael Sean Milligan. Curse! Now I'm a bloody uncle!

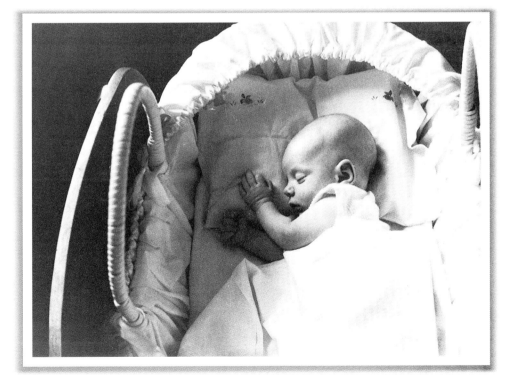

At Christmas in far-off Woy Woy, my mother reported swimming in a shark-proof enclosure. My father further avoided sharks and kept his wig dry by stopping at home. He celebrated by firing one of his muskets. Didn't the neighbours mind? A saying by my father: 'There are two things in life you can do without – Neighbours and Piles!' I had both.

Christmas for Mum and Dad in Australia meant roasting hot weather, but they still had the traditional full Christmas lunch. They were joined by Desmond, Nadia and Nadia's mother, Mrs Klun, whose name sounds like custard hitting a wall.

1966

For some time now, Desmond had been doing it to Nadia and, as expected, after nine months' wait, she delivered a boy. Desmond rushed to give him an Irish name, Michael Sean Milligan. Curse! Now I'm a bloody Uncle!

Oblomov was still packing 'em in but I'd had enough. I'd slept with three leading ladies and I called the

Below:
Cast and me drinking a farewell toast to *Oblomov*. I'm wearing the *Daily Express*.

show off. We celebrated with the cast at Maggie Jones' restaurant with three gay waiters.

17 May. Yes, yes, yes! Doing my best has paid off! Paddy had a baby girl.

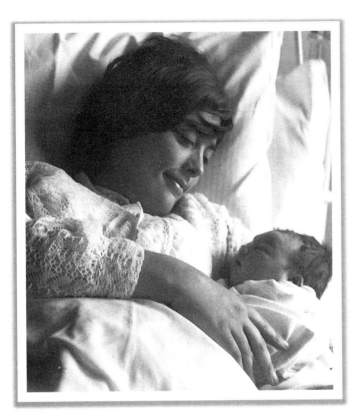

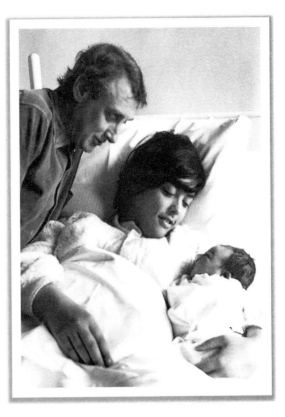

Above:
Mother and child.

Above right:
Father, mother and child.

She was to know great happiness and sorrow. I wanted to give her an Irish name like Tara, but no! The name was strangled at birth, no, no, no! It was to be an <u>English</u> name, Jane, then Fionnuala.

At first all attention was on Jane. She had to be fed at a certain time, nappy changed at a certain time, walked in the pram at a certain time, she had to go to sleep at four different times, certain time on the potty. Hadn't all this happened to me before? Was it *déjà vu*?

In distant Woy Woy, Mum was still doing her washing by hand, despite the fact that I had bought her a washing machine – she wouldn't use it!

Once, while I was visiting them at Woy Woy, I went walkabout in the bush. I came across a ruined farm with a stone inscribed, 'Dillon 1898'. There was a collapsed wooden trellis and growing amongst it was a live vine. I took a cutting and planted it in my parents' garden. After that I had come home and I received a photograph showing how remarkably well it had grown. From the grapes my mother made a wonderful jam and Dad made a box for a jar of it to be sent to me in England. The family and I found it delicious.

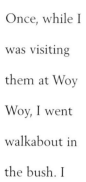

The name 'Dillon' on the stone at the farm had been quite a coincidence as it was my mother-in-law's maiden name. I also transplanted the Dillon stone to my parents' garden. Alas, time has worn it away.

In July, Laura appeared in a School

Above:
Mum not using the washing machine I bought her.

Left:
Now I'm 48! This has got to stop!

176

Right:
Breakfast and me. I had to
ring five times for it.

Below:
Silé leading a camel with
Laura and Paddy on board.

Summer Revue. By now she was a pupil at Bishop Douglas School. It was a State school and very rough. She asked me to take her away. (Eventually she went to a girls' convent.) In the show she and a friend mimed to a record and did a Charleston. She wowed 'em. Dat's my goil!

SUNSHINE GIRL ENTERS MY LIFE

Norma Farnes came to work for me on 22 August 1966. Norma became my manager and, over 30 years later, she is still with me.

Also in August, I took the whole family, less Jane (she was in the good care of a nanny), to Tunisia, the country where I had served as a soldier in World War II. We stayed in a beach bungalow at the Skanes Palace Hotel.

We drove around in a jeep, saw the Roman ruins at Dougga and the coliseum at El Djem. This was a boiling hot day and I had brought a thermos of iced water, clever me. The family were gasping when I produced it.

We swam endlessly in an azure sea. At night the kids had their supper in their bungalow. Paddy and I would go to a restaurant and be entertained by Arab belly dancers. Every evening I

177

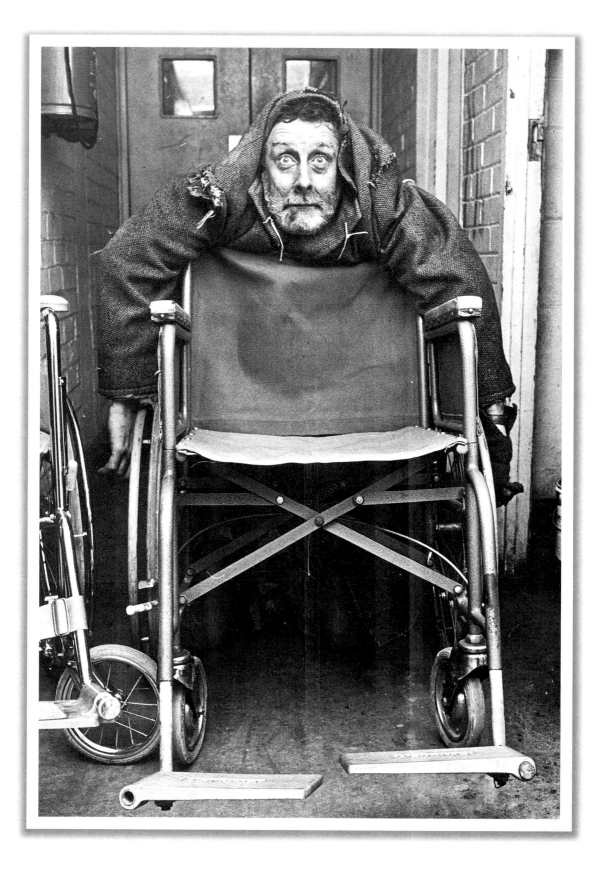

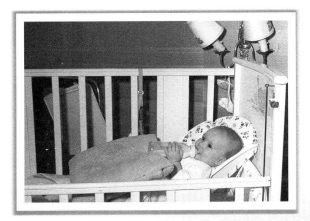

Left:
I hurt my back moving rubbish around the stage during rehearsals for *The Bed Sitting Room* in October.

Top:
Stopping for ice cream before being scared off by beggars.

Above:
Jane with a lot of bottle.

wore evening dress with a white jacket. One particular night, Paddy and I watched a very pretty Berber woman dance; she seemed interested in <u>me!</u> I was very brown with a trimmed white beard. I still retained my good looks (and modesty). The woman chose to dance around only me. I'm sure she fell for me – if only the bloody family hadn't been with me, I would be living in the desert with a Berber belly dancer now!

Paddy and the kids went to stay the night at a Troglodyte Bedouin Hotel at Qatara, where the rooms were caves, hacked out of the earth. The Eighth Army had fought their way past this place.

I took off on my own to find our original gun positions at El Aroussa. Following a map, I arrived at El Aroussa Station. From there I went on and drove across the very spot where our gun had been. The place was full of ghosts and very disturbing. 'Never go back,' they say. And they're right.

One morning we took a horse-drawn Victoria and drove all around the village of Skanes. We stopped for ice creams but, as we sat at the café, Arab beggars surrounded us, all looking alarmingly evil. We upped

and left, sad that a glorious day like that can be marred in such a way. Holiday over, we arrived home to Jane having her bottle.

On 2 December it was Silé's ninth birthday – great excitement! She wanted to dress up as a fairy, so I had to hare up to the High Street with her measurements to a fancy dress shop. I returned with the costume, which Silé then wore all day. Paddy fed Jane and made a birthday cake. Silé's present was a <u>Giant</u> Panda, which would keep company the smaller one she was to get at Christmas.

1967

On 22 April, Paddy and I went to Paris to celebrate my birthday, which had actually been (as it always is) on 16 April. 22 April is, in fact, closer to Adolf Hitler's birthday. Nevertheless, we were

Left:
Silé's birthday. Lucky she'll be getting more presents on Christmas Day.

Below:
With Bill Kerr in *The Bed Sitting Room*.

NEW HOPES AND NEW BEGINNINGS

Above:
Waiting for the Gates Of Hell
to open.

Above right:
Johnny Vyvyen, Suzan
Skupinski, Bill Kerr and Jimmy
Phillips (stage manager) on
tour with *The Bed Sitting Room*.

celebrating mine. We stayed in the Hotel Claridge, Avenue de Champs Elysées. We went to the opera and saw *Rigoletto* – very good save one character in tights. When he sang a high note he stood on his toes, causing his calf muscles to bunch up just behind his knee. I had to stifle my laughter. That night we dined at Maxim's. Alas, they put us in a corridor and we were constantly disturbed by waiters going back and forth. Our waiter was a

miserable bastard and spoilt the evening. *Vive la France* – and fuck him!

Next day we went to the Jeu de Pomme and saw Van Gogh paintings, wondrous! Hard to believe he painted them with only one ear.

Then we went on to Rodin's house with the wonderful Gates of Hell doors. His home was full of sculpture. We all know 'The Kiss'. Why did they have to take all their clothes off to do it?

In the evening we went to the

181

haunt of Jazz musicians, *Le Club Hot de France*. There were some very good musicians, great swing music.

We had to go home some time, so that's just what we did.

In May, *The Bed Sitting Room* went on tour, starting at the Saville Theatre. We toured all the main cities in England very successfully. After the show in Liverpool, we went to The Cavern of Beatles fame. I sang a scat chorus of blues with a group. I went down to shouts of MORE!!!!!

On 17 May it was Jane's first birthday. Some of her little friends came round for a party and we bought her a brightly coloured rattle, a new dress, a cake with one candle, some squeaky toys and a push trolley.

Paddy and the family went on a caravan holiday to Italy with a family friend, Mrs Kashuski and her family.

It wasn't a success. We also acquired a new Scottish nanny.

Above:
Jane takes a walk on her birthday.

Above:
Jean and Silé in her first Communion dress.

She joined us on Silé's first Communion Day. Her name was Mrs Jean Reid.

In October I flew to Australia to stay with my mum and dad for a while. This time I bought them a TV set. One evening my father, a fascist and racist, saw a corroboree on the screen. 'Who are all those niggers?' he said.

'Dad, that's a corroboree.'

'They should never have let them into the country.'

He was a peculiar man. One morning he woke me at 2 o'clock.

'What is it?' I asked.

'I've never shot a tiger,' he said.

'Why tell me?'

'I've *got* to tell somebody!'

I visited Eric Worrell's Wildlife Park and was introduced to some of Australia's native animals. I also went walkabout in the bush near Gosford. I came upon a convict-built stone house. On the verandah there was a wooden bench engraved with the initials, 'H. K.' I remembered reading an early poet called Henry Kendall who wrote *Bellbird* and *Names Upon A Stone*. Asking questions locally, I found that building had once been an inn called The Red Cow, built on a creek (now dry) where ships would anchor. The Red Cow was run by the Fagan brothers who had indeed taken Henry Kendall in as a lodger.

All this information I passed to

Sir Charles Moses, head of the ABC. I asked if he would let me do a half hour on television to raise funds for the building's restoration. He agreed, so, along with my father, we read Kendall's verse and appealed for funds. In fact, the programme raised about £3,000. I handed this to the Brisbane Historical Society who used the money for the restoration of The Red Cow. Good

Above:

Me with a native Australian.

Right:

Me as *Beachcomber*, suspecting a plot!

deed for the day. Herewith a verse from *Bellbirds*:

> *By shadows of coolness the echoes are calling*
>
> *And down the dim gorges I hear the falling:*
>
> *It lives in the mountains where moss and the sedges*
>
> *Touch with their beauty the banks and the ledges*
>
> *Through breaks of the cedar and sycamore bowers*
>
> *Struggles the light that is love to the flowers*
>
> *And softer than slumber, and sweeter than singing*
>
> *The notes of the bellbirds are running and ringing.*

There must be some mistake. The BBC want me to play the part of

Beachcomber on TV. Is it a plot? Six shows were transmitted late Autumn, so it wasn't a plot after all! The show was scripted by Neil Shand and me. It didn't break any windows. It wasn't meant to, it was meant to entertain!

In November I received a letter from Lord Montague inviting me to

drive a 1909 De Dion car in the London to Brighton old crocks race. I said I would be glad to. We were told to assemble at the Cumberland Hotel where we would be served with

and Paddy as co-driver, we set off.

All went well until about half way when the radiator started to boil over. An attendant came. 'You'll have to keep filling it up with water.' 'Is that all?' I asked. That was all. Our progress was woefully slow. It was getting on for dusk, then we were heading downhill into Brighton when the brakes failed. The momentum got us down to the esplanade and I switched off the engine. There was not a bloody soul there to greet us. Lord Montague

Left:
The family about to embark in the dreaded De Dion.

breakfast, and so we were. We were also asked to pay.

Then, with the kids in the back

Above:
I appeared on BBC 2 on Boxing Day telling *The Sad Happy Ending Story Of The Bald Twit Lion*.

demolished). I asked the porter if we could have porridge in our room at 8 o'clock. Next morning there was a knock at the door.

'Who is it?' I asked.

'It's the porridge.'

had waited, but when it started to get dark, he had gone home. So we had to take a taxi to the station and a train back to London, followed by another taxi back to Holden Road. The kids loved it. A medal to commemorate the occasion was posted to me. A month later it was stolen. What's it all about, Alfie?

In the last week in November, Paddy and I went to Dublin and stayed at the Hibernian Hotel (now

We went to the Abbey Theatre to see *Juno and the Paycock*. The Irish players were marvellous. Afterwards we had dinner at the Celtic Mews Restaurant. It was wonderful being in my own country.

There was one weird, and yet typically Irish, incident. It happened in Grafton Street. Paddy and I were strolling, looking at the shops – this was the Bond Street of Dublin. All at once,

I heard the sound of a harp playing 'The Lark Ascending'. Where on earth was it coming from? Finally, we found an elderly lady playing in a shop doorway – sitting playing a harp in a shop doorway! I was so stunned, I said to her, 'That was beautiful.' I thanked her and gave her £5. She said, 'Ta! I'm here every Friday!'

Oh, it's Christmas again! I mean, we only had one a year ago! Jane was given a junior trampoline. She surprised herself by jumping up and down. 'Look at me!' she cried excitedly, before falling off.

This was not the happiest of Christmases. I was mentally ill and had to go to bed. Since the war, I had been plagued with Manic Depression. I was in and out of psychiatric hospitals most of my life until I took Lithium. It was my salvation. Thank God for it, although he didn't suggest it. A Doctor Bott did.

Despite the illness, I was playing Ben Gunn again at The Mermaid Theatre. I took hours to put on the make-up. Not one critic mentioned it, so I packed it in a small box and addressed it to Adolf Hitler, Berlin. The last night of the show is one for jokes. Barry Humphries was playing Long

Above left:
All together with the Christmas tree and Jane's trampoline.

Above:
Nanna inspecting the damage after the fall.

Right:
Me as Benn Gunn.

John Silver. When he saw me, he said,

'It's a hippy!'

'Yes!' I said. 'And here's my flower!'

I shook my old flintlock pistol and

it released a blast of flour, blotting

him out.

1968

16 April – my 50th Birthday! This has

got to stop! Paddy bought me an

antique Victorian tie pin. The children

bought me a vintage bottle of Chateau

Margaux, 1947. I laid it down. It didn't

get up. Years later I drank it at

Christmas. It laid me down. I took all

the children save Jane to the GPO

Tower revolving restaurant. How did

the waiters ever remember which table

they were serving? Afterwards, we all

went to see *Annie Get Your Gun*. What

a wonderful score by Irving Berlin,

and funny, too.

In May Peter Sellers, having married

his dream girl, Britt Eckland, invited

Prince Charles to lunch with The

Goons at Peter's house. Secombe had

a moustache and a goatee beard as he

was appearing in *The Four Musketeers*.

He was all four of them.

Alas, Peter's marriage didn't last

long. I was present one day when she

came back from a shopping trip. He

eyed her with distaste. She threw a pair

Left:
Birthday dinner in the Post
Office Tower – I'm 50!

Top right:
Prince of Wales with *The Goons*

Bottom right:
Me and Britt Eckland, ignore
the rest.

of golf cuff links down on his table. The atmosphere was terrible, so I said, 'I've got to leave now, my house is on fire,' and went.

Dick Lester, the bald film director whose films with the Beatles had been a roaring success, wanted me to appear in a film of *The Bed Sitting Room* in June. He wanted it rewritten by his favourite writer, John Woods, who I didn't think was in the same league of comedy writers that John Antrobus and I were. There were some silly, unexplainable jokes where Michael Horden said, 'I've forgotten to put any wooden planks up my back,' before getting into bed. The film won a peace award in Russia. I enjoyed doing it and some bits of the original play were left in, but the stage show had been hilarious and I was sad that the film wasn't. Still, it was a good try by Lester.

In July Laura was voted head girl of St Mary's Abbey School and won the school prize for Senior Art. She also won the drama award!

On Anzac Day in Woy Woy, the veterans paraded in a march past and Captain L. A. Milligan marched with them.

After the parade, they all gathered at the Returned Soldiers' Club and proceeded to get blotto, except for the Captain who came home sober. What was wrong with the man?

In August I was back in Australia for my parents' 54th Wedding Anniversary. We had dinner in the kitchen. I had bought them a bottle of champagne (master of the obvious).

'Dad, have some,' I said.

'Well, the doctor said I shouldn't,' he said, 'but what the hell!'

So he took a sip, and suddenly his

Above:
Filming *The Bed Sitting Room.*

Left:
Laura as Romeo.

Below:
Old soldiers never die. Well, this lot haven't.

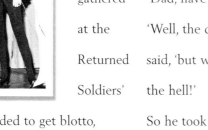

Above:

Rehearsing for a TV version of *The Goon Show* which never came to pass.

head slumped forward. Suppose the doctor was right? He began to recover a little, but he was still dopey. I took the back of his chair and dragged him to his bedroom. He managed to get his pyjamas on and get into bed.

In the morning he was still dopey. I phoned for an ambulance and Desmond and I got him into it. He kept saying how good it was to have 'two strong sons.' He would never come home again.

I visited him in Gosford Hospital. He was paralysed down his left side. They had rigged up a sling to enable him to try to lift himself up and down.

He spoke quite clearly and asked Mum to buy him some dates. He was

worried about his bowel movements. I saw him every day for a week and then I had to get back home for some bloody job. Dad was moved to Newcastle

Hospital bloody miles away. Desmond would drive the 120 miles with Mum on weekends. But Dad deteriorated.

My family knew little of this as they were all holidaying in Tobago. They travelled by a banana boat, M.V. *Golfito*.

1969

In February came a very sad day for me. I received a telegram from my mother:

FATHER VERY ILL. HE MAY GO

ANY TIME.

LOVE MUM AND DES.

Top left:
Silé, Paddy and Jane, the Coke freak, rafting on the Rio Grande river.

Top right:
Jane, the beach baby.

Left:
My father's coffin.

Next day, Dad was dead. At his funeral, a police car led the way. He had been a wonderful father. I shall miss him as long as I live.

It was years since I had written *The Goon Shows*, but it was only after they finished that I received a copy of the newsletter from *The Goon Show Preservation Society*. Evidently it had been going, as I had been, for years. The Patron was Prince Charles and they were extremely well organised with branches as far distant as Australia, Canada, America and South Africa.

Above:
Mum, Desmond and mourners follow the coffin.

Below:
With Ringo Starr and Peter Sellers in *The Magic Christian*.

The Society is still going strong today. This year also saw the publication of another book, *The Bedside Milligan*. Apparently it didn't reach many bedsides. I had quite a few by my bedside, about a hundred, which I sold for a new bed.

Laura went to her first ball this winter and, therefore, had to have her first ball gown. She looked so grown up!

Above:
With Eric Sykes in Johnny Speight's *Curry And Chips*.

Right:
Laura in her first ball gown.

AFRICA, ISRAEL AND MONKENHURST

1970

In March I was back in Africa making a commercial for the tourist industry in Kenya. When it was finished, I arranged for Jane and Paddy to join me and go on safari. When Paddy and Jane arrived, we went for a walk to let Jane (then aged four) get accustomed to her new surroundings. We passed a beggar with only one leg. I gave the poor chap a pound. I let Jane hand him the money.

'Yes, wid dat money he can buy a new leg.' Lump in throat.

After a night of violent thunderstorms at Sayonara camp which were accompanied by the distant roaring of lions, Jane had much to say. 'Can lions kill you?'

'Yes, Jane, they can.'

'Do they kill people when they roar?'

'No, darling. I suppose when they're roaring they can't eat.'

The magnificent beach at Malindi
and me from the waist up.

'Can they kill you a lot? Last night we heard lions roaring, didn't we Mummy?'

'Yes, but they were a long way away.'

'Were they killing someone?'

On 12 March we visited Olduvai Gorge, where Dr Leakey had discovered fossilised animals' bones dating back millions of years. The gorge was an ancient sight of early Man, Australo Pithicus, and a treasure trove for budding archeologists like me. From an axe 'factory' I recovered a stone axe and from the same site the hip bone of a giant gorilla. Imagine stretching your mind back 90 million years. I tried to stretch mine back but could only reach 1931.

Driving back to camp, we saw young white rhinos. This species had been saved by a man called Harry Player, whom we went to visit. His home was way out in the bush – 'far out, man'. His manservant was an old Zulu and I recalled that my great grandfather, Trumpet Major Alfred Kettleband, had been in the battle which took place on the Plains of Isandlwana when the Zulus wiped out an army of British Redcoats, my great grandfather being one of them. When Player informed his Zulu servant of this, he replied that his great granfather had also been in the battle! As we got into our Jeep to leave, the Zulu stood on a mound, calling out that I was the son of a son of a great warrior who fought on that distant day.

Above:
Jane at a safe distance.

Below:

Jane and me fossicking in the ancient ruins of an abandoned Arab town.

Below right:

Monkey business.

I asked Player to thank him and say I was glad I hadn't been there personally.

One early morning, Paddy saw Jane talking to a young vervet monkey. 'He was a baby,' she explained. 'He was trying to talk, but he couldn't.'

We travelled on to William Holden's luxury Kenya Safari Club at the foot of Mount Kilimanjaro. We were in a stone-built lodge with every modern convenience – marble bath, gold taps. 'Can we take one, Mummy?'

On the lawn strutted albino peacocks. There was a stone fireplace which crackled with logs in the cool evenings. Dinner was served by white-coated waiters. I asked one his name.

'Sam,' he said.

'No, what is your tribal name?'

'N(click)gongo.'

Christian society has a lot to answer for. Swirling over the peak of Kilimanjaro were heavy mists. I told Jane it was the abode of witches, he-he-he-he-he . . .

One night we requested a Zulu meal of 'mealie'. It consisted of a kind of coarse flour made from maize and corn cobs. This formed a circular wall with meat in the middle. I was, by then,

Top left:
Jane outside the hut the morning after thunderstorms and the roaring of distant lions.

Below:
Last photo of the holiday!

spent the last days of the holiday swimming and sunbathing. It had been wonderful for Jane to see Africa through a child's eyes. Mine were too red.

On 29 March, we returned to London.

Oh, dear.

My mother and her friend, Muriel (a bit too loud for me), took a trip on the MV *Fairstar* from Sydney to Southampton and spent some time with us.

a vegetarian, but what the hell! I'd never have the same opportunity again. With the mealie I drank a glass of Zulu beer. God, it was strong stuff! We sat aroung the log fire dreaming dreams in the flames. That night came the distant sound of drums. I told Jane the drums were to frighten the witches from their lair, he-he-he-he . . .

On 25 March, we took a flight to Malindi. A car then took us on to the Seafarers Lodge at Watama. There was a magnificent beach and we were installed in a hut right by the sea. We

Above left:

Mum trying to steer the ship to the amusement of the Captain.

Middle:

The music hall cast including Peter Sellers, Keith Michell and Ronnie Barker.

Above right:

D Battery Band reunited. (*L to R*) Harry Edgington, me, A. C. Fildes, Doug Kidgell.

In October, the BBC decided to stage an old-style variety bill at the Wilton Music Hall, using recreations of original music hall acts. I played E. W. Mackney a coloured American and the cast was a star-studded affair, even including Peter Sellers!

In November, there was a reunion at the Printers Devil in Fetter Lane for D Battery, 56 Heavy Regiment. All of the members of the D Battery Band were there. We used to be *The Beatles* of Bexhill. We played some great swing music, including our old favourite, 'Honeysuckle Rose'.

1971

In January, the first volume of my war memoirs, *Adolf Hitler, My Part In His Downfall*, was published and became a big success. It went on and on reprinting and, almost 30 years later, it is still in print and still selling. Thank God! The money! There was a lavish party on publication after which I took the whole family to Kettner's Restaurant. I gave the children half a glass of wine and Sean ended up under the table.

My frenetic diary for October shows me flying to Australia on the 9th. I left the children in the care of Paddy and their nanny. There are no entries until Tuesday 12th, then just one word 'Studio'. Was it radio or TV? One or the other. I really can't remember. There's nothing else in the diary until 19 November when it says 'Post material for BBC'. Had I really come to Australia to write for <u>them</u>?

Possibly. The first of the Q series had been launched a couple of years before and it had really caused a stir. In writing the series, I abandoned the notion that a show or even a sketch had to have a set form. This was free-form comedy. We would just end a sketch with everyone pacing towards the camera saying 'What are we goin' to do now?' with each step. Then we were straight into the next one. It really shook up the Pythons when they first saw it. Without Q there would have been no Python. They'd tried. They tried with *At Last The 1948 Show*.

Far left:
Appearing in Marty Feldman's TV show.

Above:
Publication party for *Adolf Hitler, My Part In His Downfall.*

They didn't know that you could have a show with no beginnings, with no

across the Rip to explore the other side. I found what was obviously an old aboriginal trail up the rocks. At the top, on a flat surface, were lots of aborigine carvings. Fish (baramundi), dingos, sharks and numerous kangaroos. Below the flat ledge was a cave. I leant on a rock shelf with a surface of wind-blown sand. Brushing the rock clear, I revealed a remarkable carving of men in a rowing boat. Aborigines <u>don't</u> row, they paddle. What I was looking at was a boat full of English sailors rowing up the rip with Captain Phillips, who explored this stretch of coast in the 1700s. I reported the cave and carvings to Professor John Clegg at Sydney University. He excavated the cave. Its occupation went back 600 years.

Above:
Paddy at the Earl's Court Boat Show. Like me, Paddy campaigned for animal rights and was photographed on this cabin cruiser with simulated tiger skin furnishings.

ends, with interruptions. Q really did break new ground.

One day in Woy Woy, I took a boat

I travelled on to New Zealand in

Left:
Me with three native Australians at Eric Worrel's wild life park.

Below:
Edgington warning me that the moment I return to England I will be unemployed.

November to visit Harry Edgington, who had fled to Wellington to escape what he called the impending giant unemployment crisis in England, which never really came. I took the Edgingtons to dinner and sampled New Zealand 'whitebait' which looked like fried maggots. Although a vegetarian, I partook of the lamb. The New Zealand red burgundy we drank had a kick like a mule. But I've never been kicked by a mule, so how do I know?

I flew back to England on 7 December and, looking back through my diary, the rest of the month is mostly blank. Ominously, many pages have ILL written in large letters.

Above:

Dinner at the Post Office Tower Restaurant.

Below right:

Two photographs of Laura partially out of her mind.

1972

Come 16 April, I was 54. We all went for dinner at the Post Office Tower Restaurant.

Afterwards I took the family to Ronnie Scott's where the great Duke Ellington tenor player, Ben Webster, was playing. It was magic!

Laura went to Newcastle to stay with a friend, Margaret Maugham, who took photographs of her in various costumes. The pictures looked very arty, if a little strange . . .

Our summer holiday this year was in Malta, staying at the Hilton Hotel. Oh, the money!!

My room had everything I needed. I had put up the library shelves and started to collect books, mostly auto-biographies, biographies and books on war. The walls were hung with my children's paintings. I had an intercom which connected to every room, a telephone, a radio and a TV set. I have always been a telly addict and it was luxury for me to be able to lie in bed and watch TV.

On New Year's Eve, Paddy and I sat up to greet the New Year I couldn't bring myself to sing 'Should Auld Aquaintance'. We drank a toast and then went to bed – she to hers and I to mine. I have always, even when married, slept in my own bedroom.

Left:
Malta – yes, Jane went snorkelling.

Below:
This lot are costing me a fortune!

1973

In the spaces between living and other work, I continued to write my war memoirs. Each of the books would become a bestseller!

Above:
My bedroom. It had everything
I needed.

Above right:
My God! Silé is 15! Is there no
way of stopping it?

Right:
The whole family on *This Is
Your Life*. Oh, the expense!

On 6 April, the D Battery reunion was held at the De La War building in Bexhill (the ugliest building in England). Surprise, surprise! Waiting for me was Eammon Andrews and 'Spike Milligan, tonight, This Is Your Life!' I was nonplussed, flabbergasted. My first comment was, 'You call this *living*?' There followed surprise after surprise. All of my family was there, including my mother all the way from Australia with Desmond and Nadia. Peter Sellers came dressed as a German soldier and denied all knowledge of me. Eric Sykes admitted he had heard of me, the swine. Harry Secombe overwhelmed me with praise and ended with a raspberry to which I replied tenfold. This must have cost the TV company a fortune. What the hell, I was worth it!

209

16 April. My bloody birthday <u>again</u>! I'm now fifty-bloody-five! So, a giant dinner party at Kettner's in a private room. All the family – Mum, Des

and Nadia with Michael, all there

thanks to the TV company. Shortly after, Mum had to depart for Australia. When would she see us all again? Never? We lived in hope with an overdraft!

That summer, my son Sean begged me to buy him a motorbike. Christ, was there no end to it? So I bought him a bloody motorbike. Three months later he wanted to sell it. I asked why. 'Because I'm going to kill myself if I go on riding it!' So he sold it and kept the bloody money!

Also that summer, Dick Lester asked me to play a part in his movie *The Three Musketeers*. I played the aged husband of a young Raquel Welch! I got really good notices, especially in

Left:
Royal Premiere of the film *Alice's Adventures In Wonderland*. Fiona Fullerton was Alice, I played the Gryphon and Peter was the March Hare. I had accidentally shot myself in the hand!

Far left :
Farewell dinner. Goodbye, Mum.

Above:
Me, Dick Lester and God knows who.

Top right:
Paddy and Jane with an unnamed statue.

Bottom right:
Laura looking for buried treasure.

Doloroso. We stood before the ancient Wailing Wall where Jane wrote a message and put it in a crack in the wall. I often wonder what it was that she wrote.

In Haifa we visited the Garden of Remembrance and the museum which showed the horrors of the Holocaust. I was glad when we left there. We went to the ruins of ancient Caesare and fossicked for bits

America. The result? Fuck all.

For years Dr Joe and Charlotte Robson had been my good friends. He was a psychiatrist treating me for a sleep problem. One of his sons, Jeremy, I put on the path to becoming a publisher and he has become a real success! It was the Robsons who prompted me to visit Israel. In August we flew out to stay in the Dan Hotel in Tel Aviv. In Jerusalem we walked in the footsteps of Jesus along the Via

with the presence of Jesus. I swam in the Dead Sea to see if it still was. All you could do was float. It amused my children no end.

When we went to Bethlehem, I couldn't believe that I was actually there. We saw the alleged birthplace of Jesus. I wonder?

Israel's state of awareness was obvious by the number of Israeli troops in the towns but that didn't detract from an unforgettable holiday – a very emotional experience.

In October, Robson Books (yes, Joe's son!) threw a party to celebrate the publication of the second volume

Left:
Jane with her birthday cake, made by Paddy!

from the past. I found a wall of biblical rubbish including the base of a 'tear cup', in which women with menfolk who were away at war collected tears to show them when they returned.

We went out in a boat on the Sea of Galilee, the waters all around alive

Right:

Silé, ready at last, with her escort.

Right:

Silé, ready at last, with her escort.

Below:

Secombe trying to draw attention to himself at the Robson Books party.

of *The Goon Show* scripts. This brought me the largest royalty earnings I had had up to that point – £18,000, folks!

Also this month Silé was to have her first ball gown. Paddy did a lot of measuring up, we let Silé choose the material, a pale yellow silk. She was so excited the night before the ball that she couldn't sleep. The next evening all efforts were concentrated on:

a) getting Silé's hair done

b) half an hour on make-up.

c) The Gown. Her escort arrived in evening dress, I can't recall his name. Shall we say he is Dick Turnbull? Why not? That, at least, is how I remember it all, but looking back at the photograph of Laura's first ball gown, they seem remarkably similar. The same dress?

For God's sake don't tell Silé!

I received a phone call from Kyrenia, Cyprus, from a worried producer. He was making a film called *A Ghost In The Noonday Sun* starring Peter Sellers and Tony Francioso. Peter didn't like the script and wanted me to come and rewrite it. I read the original

script. It was absolute crap, really just a remake of *Treasure Island*. I flew to Kyrenia and was put in an inn called The Harp. I immediately had to start work on the script. No one cast in the film was capable of any kind of humorous performance except Peter. All I wrote was destroyed. It was all a complete nightmare, but it was a very lovely spot with Greek and Turkish restaurants along the harbour. I flew Paddy, Jane, Silé and Laura to join me in The Harp. Every morning I bought fresh loaves from a Turkish bakery – warm bread stuffed with dates! The family loved Cyprus.

We were all home again for Christmas week. Paddy and I rushed to finish the Christmas tree which, when loaded with decorations, fell over. We kept it upright by putting rocks around it, although I really felt like throwing the rocks <u>at</u> it.

Above:
With Florilyn Waddell in *Milligan In Spring*, one of four seasonal TV shows I made for the BBC.

Right:

Maggie Jones handled the catering on the nightmare movie in Cyprus.

Below left:

The family around the Christmas tree, Jane happily sucking her thumb.

Below right:

Jane distressed. Bloody adults! Paddy told her to stop sucking her thumb!

A typical family Christmas followed: rows, breaking crockery, setting fire to the Christmas tree.

1974

I was commissioned by *The Times* to cover a game of backgammon on board the *Queen Mary* sailing to New York and back. My article was entitled 'There And Backgammon'. During the trip I swam in the heated swimming pool and relaxed, so much so that when a young

I left my lungs in Dublin Zoo

With you

I left my teeth on Table Mountain

High on a hill they smile at me

When I go back to San Francisco

There won't be much for them to see.

I returned to Australia to finish another volume of war memoirs – the fourth; *Mussolini, His Part In My Downfall*. Mum looked after me well. She bought beautiful organic vegetables with such variety (Australia – land of plenty) and one evening made a marvellous curry. One evening? She had spent all day on it. We had a civilised dinner with Desmond, sitting on the

Left:

Me recovering from the young girl's visit on the *Queen Mary*.

Below:

The ten-day *Queen Mary* trip meant I was away for my birthday, so my lovely Jane laid on a special late birthday party on my return.

woman came into my cabin and said, 'Would you like a quickie?' I was too stunned to say yes!

In July I did a one-man show, one-man that is, except for the other man, a South African singer called Jeremy Taylor. He sang and played the guitar like a maestro. I liked to end the show with 'San Francisco':

I left my heart in San Francisco

I left my knees back in Peru

I left my little wooden leg

Hanging on a peg

Above left:

Silé dressed to kill. I wonder who the victim is?

Above right:

Jane appeared in a school play as an Egyptian soldier at the time of Tutankhamen. She repeated her performance for me at home.

Right:

Recalling the good old days, Mum and me make a toast to Captain L. A. Milligan, Royal Artillery.

verandah by oil lamp, talking of Mum and Dad's early days. They had enjoyed such a good lifestyle in India. The disappointments of England could be written off. Here in Australia they had a very happy retirement. I recalled Leo's constant efforts to get money for nothing. He once wrote to his Masonic Lodge Headquarters saying he was down on his luck and could they give him some 'assistance'. Eventually, a letter arrived saying that a member of Sydney Lodge would visit him to establish his circumstances. No date was given. The member arrived on Leo's birthday, for which I had sent him a box of Havana cigars and a case of half a dozen bottles of Heidsieck Dry Monopole Champagne. The Masonic visitor came to see the 'impoverished' Leo sitting on the verandah smoking a cigar and drinking champagne! The previous year I had written *Badjelly The Witch*. I wrote it longhand in a very good, painstaking, calligraphic style to encourage

youngsters to learn how to write. The book did very well and, astoundingly, in far off New Zealand we had several requests to turn it into a school play.

New Zealand was where I was bound next, flying from Sydney to Wellington, where I stayed with Harry Edgington. I took my cornet with me and we relived those years when we were the darlings of Bexhill. We weren't as good as we had been then, but just as enthusiastic.

Back in England there was a property boom. When I arrived home in September, half the houses in Holden Road had been sold at a huge profit. David White was a speculator who was desperate for me to sell 127. I had bought it for £3,500 and was being offered £30,000 for it. I didn't want to sell. It was the first home I had ever owned and I knew that, if I sold, the house would be pulled down for redevelopment. One day David drove

Top:
Edgington and I reliving the war years in a confined space.

Above:
Compering ABC TV's *This Day Tonight.*

September, 1974

Mr. and Mrs. Spike Milligan
wish to inform you
that their new address is

MONKENHURST
THE CRESCENT
HADLEY COMMON
HERTFORDSHIRE

TELEPHONE 440 0091

Above:
The change of address card
Paddy had printed.

Right:
Monkenhurst boasted a
marvellous Adam fireplace in
the drawing room.

me to Hadley Wood and he pointed to a beautiful Victorian Manor. He said, 'I'll give you this for yours.' I couldn't resist it. We moved from 127, sadly, late in September. It broke my heart but what we were getting was a sumptuous property – Monkenhurst. I spent £10,000 restoring it. In the drawing room was a marvellous Adam fireplace and the house was eventually voted one of the beautiful private dwellings of London by the Institute of Architects. I was proud to live in such a wonderful building. Christmas in Monkenhurst was a fabulous affair. Our Christmas tree was the biggest ever. The ceilings in Monkenhurst were very high, so we had a tree to fit. How do trees have fits?

Right on cue, it snowed and we had a happy Christmas week. Most of my presents were bottles of wine. Paddy bought me a dozen bottles of Orvieto Abbrocado. This is one of my favourites, a wine which I first discovered in Italy during the war. We were in a gun position at Lauro. I was an O.P. signaller and we were supporting the Hampshire Regiment who were to attack the village of Orvieto. At dawn they took the objective, a typical village with a

square and a fountain in the centre. Then we were subjected to a storm of German artillery. We took shelter in the cellars around the square. In these cellars were barrels of wine. We soon filled our water bottles. In fact, we emptied them and refilled them several times. When the shelling ended, the Hampshires lolled about the square, me amongst them. A Jeep arrived with a Colonel Simpson, their commanding officer. He went up to a pissed sergeant, kicked him in the boot.

'You!' he said. 'Do you know who I am?'

The sergeant turned to his buddy and

Above:

Monkenhurst in the snow.

Above:
The family and the biggest tree ever..

Right:
Jane in her new Christmas coat, on her way to show it to her friend, Nelly Ninnis.

became very sad. Don't ask me why. Perhaps it was the memory of my own childhood Christmases.

There were certainly worse Christmases ahead. In the very near future Paddy was to develop breast cancer. Eventually she had the breast removed and wore a mould. She was given the all-clear in 1977 but the cancer reappeared in her spine and upper neck. She went to see a naturopath who had 'cured his own cancer'. Amongst other things, he said we must remove all vapour-producing medicines in the house – Vick's etc. Our usual doctor, Dr Thurman, visited her from time to time to

said, 'There's a cunt here doesn't know who he is!'

The wine was Orvieto Abbrocado and now, thirty years later, I had a dozen bottles to drink. I drank a bottle of it with Christmas lunch. Despite everything, over the Christmas period I

try to persuade her to take a normal anti-cancer treatment but she refused, and gradually she declined. I never told Jane that Paddy was going to die until the day before it happened.

I said, 'Darling, Mummy's dying.'

She said, 'No, she'll be better by Christmas.'

I said, 'No, darling.'

She said, 'But I'm only eleven!'

Oh, God, the pain.

Jane has grown up the double of her mother. She has taken to the stage, sings, dances, plays keyboards and saxophone as well as classical flute. How proud her mother would have been of her.

1975

In February I was taken to Rhodesia to do a commercial for the tourist industry. After I had finished it, I had

the front door. I opened it. It was a policeman. 'Excuse me, sir. There's a car parked in the main road unattended.' I told him I had no knowledge of it. 'Oh, sorry to have bothered you, sir. Good night.' He was totally unmoved by my appearance.

Above:
Paddy with a thief trying to steal her necklace at the Wankie Game Lodge.

Left:
A cherry tree blossomed when 127 Holden road was demolished by a bulldozer. I had it replanted at Monkenhurst but, after blooming, it died. I planted a new one.

Right:
Soaked! But the Victoria Falls were unbelievable. We saw the famous rainbow and, that night, a moonbow!

enough money to fly Paddy, Jane, Laura, Silé, Sean and the nanny out for a tour of the wild places. We travelled overland by Jeep to the Wankie Game Lodge. Venturing forth from the camp early every morning, we went in search of animals. Another wonderful holiday.

For Jane's ninth birthday, there was a big party at Monkenhurst. What a mad house. All her friends were there wearing 'zany' make-up. I had dressed up as Hitler. There was a knock on

Here the story must draw to a close. Having reached the age of 57 and travelled the world from India and Burma to England, Africa and Australia, I had a great deal to look back on, a great many happy memories and a great deal of sadness. There was a great deal of both still to come . . .

Left:
Party at the mad house!

Below:
My bank manager calls to enquire about the next volume of *The Family Album* . . .